LEARN PLC PROGRAMMING

Mastering Motion Control with PLCopen, Made Easy Programming PLCs for Precision Control Handbook for Engineers

By

Furuta Kimiko

TABLE OF CONTENTS

INTRODUCTION

Welcome to discourse on policy, programming motion control with policy open. Motion control is a very deep sub field of automation, extensively used for a variety of purposes and applications. And this course you will learn the both theoretical concepts regarding motion control and practical knowledge. You will learn that the PRC open standard that is the most used a worldwide motion controls standard, and you will apply it to the real world scenarios.

Using the Soft Motion Causes library, you will be able to completely simulate the motion control system without having any outdoor and completely for free. In this course, we will use the structured text language in the code system environment to learn and program motion control a simulated application within the PSC programming environment. To properly understand that the content of this course, you should have some basic knowledge of PRC programming and know the cause embarrassment.

INTRODUCTION TO MOTION CONTROL

We will talk about what motion control is, how it works, and what are the key components related to it. Motion control is a sub field of automation regarding the controlled movement of mechanical parts of the machine with a high degree of accuracy. The movement of mechanical parts is typically achieved using electric motors, motion control is typically used in different engineering fields such as manufacturing, robotics or precision engineering. Let's see now what are the components involved in motion control. We have the motion controller that is the brain of the whole process. It is a high performance industrial PC or policy whose purpose is to be programmed by a user to generate motion profiles, meaning to compute the position as piece of points for the motors handling synchronization of multiple motors when needed. This set points are sent to an electric drive. Its purpose is to supply current to the electric motor, according to the path that the motion controller is requesting.

Motion Control Components

• **Electric Motor:** motor whose purpose is to supply torque to a mechanical load to move it.

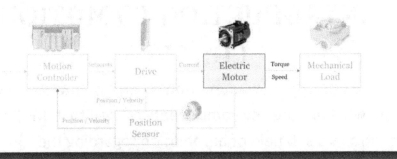

The electric motor will use the current supplied by the driver in order to generate torque and therefore mechanical motion of moving parts. Then there typically is a position sensor for the motor that will measure where the motor is and will send feedbacks to the drive and to the motion controller. Typical technologies for the position sensor are encoders or resolvers. So when people say motion control, it typically means that the programming of the motion controller in order to achieve the desired motion of the mechanical moving parts.

MOTION CONTROL MAIN VARIABLES

We will talk about the most important variables used when discrediting motion control application and technologies, which are positions, velocities, accelerations, perks and currents. Position is a variable that describes where our moving parts are related to a fixed point. It can be used to determine the rotation of the motor shaft so we could have a rotational position measured in grease or gradients, or we could have some leaner position given by the mechanics of the system for which we could use a leaner unit of measurement, such as millimetres or inches, to be generic. We will define the unit of measurement of a position as a generic unit. The position should be referred to a fixed point that will be the zero of our measurement and position can be measured in an absolute way related to the fixed point or in a relative way looking at the starting point of a movement, for example. All this consideration can also be applied to protective systems. Velocity or speed is a variable that is the derivative of position. This means that it describes how fast the position is changing. If an object is moving with a high velocity, it means that its position is changing fast wireless stand alone velocity means that its position is changing slowly.

Main Variables for Motor Control

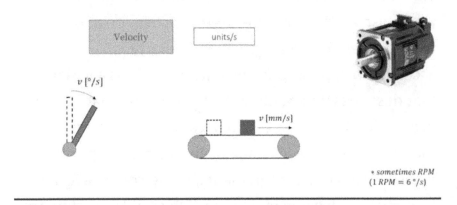

The unit of measurement of a velocity is the position unit per second, so we could have degrees per second for rotating motion or millimeters per second for a linear movement. A popular unit of measurement for velocity is the RPM or revolutions per minute that is just another way of measuring velocity. Just know that an RPM is equal to six degrees per second. Acceleration is the derivative of velocity. That means that it describes how fast the velocity of an object is changing. If an object is subjected to a stronger acceleration, it means that its velocity is changing very quickly. The unit of measurement for acceleration is unit per second squared.

Now, let's talk about talk. But first, let's look at this leaner equivalent, the force. We know by Newton's law that force equals mass times acceleration. But let's look at this equation in the following way. Acceleration equals force divided by mass. This form of the equation is actually more exploitative, and it means that the sum of all forces on an object to generate an acceleration on the object that is inversely proportional to its mass, meaning that heavy object will require more force to receive the same acceleration. So in a typical scenario, we will apply some moving force to an object and there will be some resisting force as well on it, such as friction and the difference of this force will generate an acceleration on the object. Talk is the exact same principle, but in the rotating domain, like a force at work will generate and then go that acceleration that is inversely proportional to the moment of insertion of an object around the center.

Main Variables for Motor Control

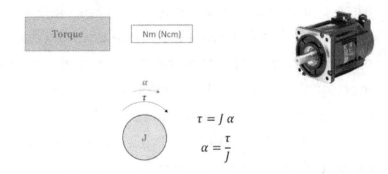

$$\tau = J\,\alpha$$

$$\alpha = \frac{\tau}{J}$$

The moment of inertia, J, is the property that depends on the mass distribution of the object that will tell us how hard it is to generate and then the acceleration of this object around its axis. So in a typical scenario, we will use a motor to apply a moving target to an object and there will be some resisting torque on the opposite to such as friction. The difference of these talks will lead it to an angle that acceleration on the object and talk is what the generates motion in the mechanical domain. And in order to generate target, we use electrical motors and electrical motors that use electrical current to generate torque. In most motor technologies, the torque generated by a motor is equal to a constant Katie times the current. So in real world applications, we will hear about current control or total control. You should know that these are practically the same after a constant demand action. So this five hour the main the main variables for motion control.

MOTION CONTROL TECHNOLOGIES

First, talking about applications in which the control of motors is involved, we can divide most technological applications according to the performance of the motion that is requested and the complexity of the comments that are sent to the electric drives and motors. We have variable speed drives application in which typically it is sufficient to control the velocity of the motors without caring about the motor position at a specific time. These kinds of applications include the ventilation, pumping and hoisting. His application feature a low level of comments, complexity and performance for the motorists involved in the movement. On the other end of the spectrum, or we have a numerical control machines, also known as ANC, that they are typically used for machining tools such as drills, lace nails and 3D printers and this kind of application. There is a relatively small number of motors that need to move together with a very high degree of precision. Motion control application for somewhere between the view of the CRC applications in motion control application, you may have many motors that needs to carry out a very precise movements. You may have a need for synchronicity of movement between different motors, but the precision needed is not as high as the ones that you would require for CSC applications.

Motor Control Applications

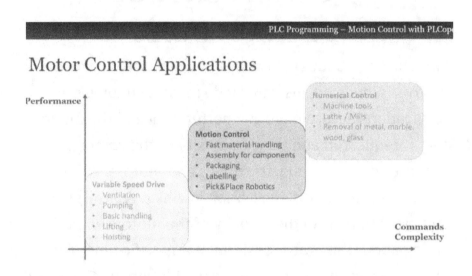

Let's now talk about the different motor technologies that can be used for motion control. A synchronous motors or induction motors are AC motors, with the current generated in the rotor to produce torque is obtained by electromagnetic induction from the state or windings. They are widely used because they are self-starting, economical and can be scaled up to big sizes with lower costs. With respect to other technologies, they are typically used for variable speed drives applications for France and France, for instance, since they are often used in application in which only speed is important. And they are also often used in an open loop control, meaning that they don't require position sensors such as an encoder to regulate the current for the motor. Versus motors are permanent magnetic signature, and those motors in which the talk is generated on the rotor through the interaction and orientation of the magnetic field on the rotor generated by magnets. And the one on this little one gives. In this motors, a closed loop controller is used to switch this equipment in the windings in order to effectively rotate the magnetic field on the data. Brushless motors are High-Performance motors that can achieve pretty high tools and speed.

Motor Technologies

Asynchronous Motors

Brushless Motors

Linear Motors

Stepper Motors

They can be position controlled with a very high degree of accuracy and are pretty expensive. Linear motors are motors that at Devastator and Rotor are rolled in a linear way. Therefore, working on a linear path, producing forces instead of talks, they're very precise and efficient because they don't use any mechanical transmission to generate a linear motion. They are very accurate and can generate big talks, but they are pretty expensive stepper motors or motors with a variable reluctance that divide a full rotation of the motor in different steps or increments. The motor can be commanded to move and all these steps without any position sensor. They are not very precise for what concerned the movement profile, but they can reach a correct final position with health using a close control stepper motors don't cost too much. And they have pretty high torque at low speeds and are frequently used for calibration applications or cerebral actuation. Motion control can be applied to all these motor technologies, but since miraculous cleaner motors are the most performing ones, they are the main focus of motion control applications.

WHAT IS A HOMING PROCEDURE

In this lesson, we will look at what a no mean procedure for next year and why it is necessary in motion control. It mean procedure is the initialization run of an axis in which the correct actual position is determined by the means of a reference signal. In many cases of motion control, when an nexus is switched on, the actual absolute position of the axis is unknown. This actually depends on the kind of position sensor that is used for the axis. For example, incremental encoders are a relative position measurement system, meaning that they cannot detect a static absolute position, but they only can detect the distance and X is as traveled. When the axis is switched down, the drive won't have any indication on the absolute position of the axis and therefore initial initialization procedure or homing is needed. Instead of absolute encoders, we can detect the absolute position of an axis. This means that in certain cases at the machine start up the electric drive, it will know the absolute position of the axis and the numbing procedure won't be necessary.

PLCopen Motion Control

PLCopen for Motion Control defines the **Function Blocks** for the different Motion Control operations.

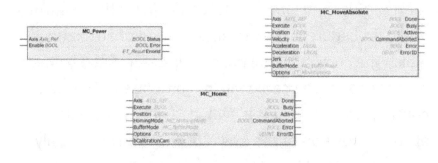

Taking into consideration that the absolute encoders ever working range, you may have a single turning colder in which the absolute position measurement can occur only within a single turn of the motor shaft or a turning quarter in which the measurement can occur upon a certain number of motor shaft terms. In any case, absolute encoders have a finite range. Therefore, if you turn on an axis while it is outside its encoder range, you may need a normal procedure as well. So typically, a normal procedure will work with a reference sensor. The axis should start moving in the direction of the sensor until the reference sensor has been found on that point. Typically, a known position value is written on the axis. These values typically zero. So in this way, if the axis moves, it will remain referenced to the initial point that you had the forming procedure.

PLCOPEN FUNCTION BLOCKS

We will talk about the standard interface and behaviour of some open motion control, some of us. See, open function books are used to control movements, diagnostics, media viewer of monitors. Its function will need to be linked to the physical access that shouldn't be controlled, so there must be a unique reference for the system so that the function lock can access it. The access to the VCR or audio configuration device, the important part is that the function blocks should be able to read from it and write it. Therefore, you need to use the open function, but the reason out variable called axis to reference this object axis after. The PRC opens tomorrow. There are two main type of function blocks. The Enable Function works and the execute function thus. He nimble social works identified by be enabled bullying of input are related to operations that persist in time since his polling on this enabled social works are also known as start stop function loss. In order to start the execution of an animal function, look, the user should set the needle input through. Then the operation will start and keep going until either an error occurs or the user sets the enable input to false. Enables function blocks and also a unified output interface with the following output variables busy. That would be true when the function clock is running and executing its purpose error. That would become true if an error is detected during the function. Mock execution and error that will contain a diagnostic code representing the error that has occurred is no error has occurred that it will maintain in zero belly. So this is what would happen on an illegal structure block when the enabling put the center through the busy output will tell us if the function is operating. And as soon as the police gets the force, the function lock will stop executing and a busy output will become force as well.

PLCopen Motion Control Function Block Interface

In the PLCopen definition, there are two main input interfaces for Motion Control Function Blocks:

Enable Function Blocks:

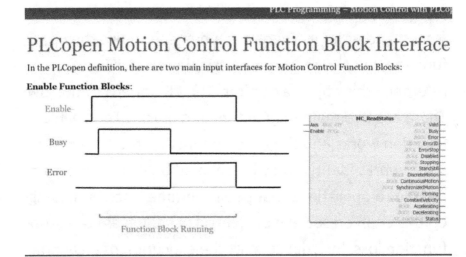

Function Block Running

Instead, if an error occurs during its operation, the busy output will become false and the function look will stop operating and the robot will become through to signal the user that the arrow could. Their output would become false again as soon as the enabling put this. Execute function instead are used for operation that do not persist in time, meaning that they have a clear start and end. They are also known as do the functional looks, and they are stocked with a rising edge of the executed input so they don't work on the current value of the input. But they will only start with rising yet. So you may have the execute people through and the operation of the function may have already ended. Also, exec function books and a unified output interface, other than the error and error, the outputs that are shared with the animal function books. They also have a gun output that will become true as soon as the operation of the function book is being completed and a command aborted output. That would become true only if the function book execution has been aborted by another function block completely the same access. So this is out, and that's a good function look will typically operate when the execute becomes through the pressure starts and after a while, it's cash this. When the operation finishes the busy output, because what was done output becomes true if the operation completed successfully. Otherwise, if another occurs, the arrow will become true whether what the BBC becomes false. Either way, this output, the done or the error were made true as long as the executing put remains through. Given the fact that exit poll function look work on raising ads, if you raise the exact info just for an impulse, the operation will start as well and work in the same way. If when the operation terminates the exit disclosed that the Dun Dun error output will become true only for a policy cycle.

SOFTMOTION LIBRARY INSTALLATION

I will show you how to get started, download and install the soft motion package of four courses. First of all, you need to have an existing courses, set up installation working on your machine, and I suggest you to have at least and an installed that is a 3.5 service pack, 15 or newer. So in order to download the soft motion package, you need to go to the Code CS dot com website and click on the store icon over here. And here in the store, you need to search for soft machine. And you can selected the first result that you get over here. And don't be alarmed. You will see your price ranging from a certain under the Euros to $475, but don't worry. This is only for the paid version and we are going to use the demo version. There is the only difference here is that the demo version can be freely used in simulation mode, and it is limited for one hour of functioning on a real machine. So for what we need in this course, the demo version is more than

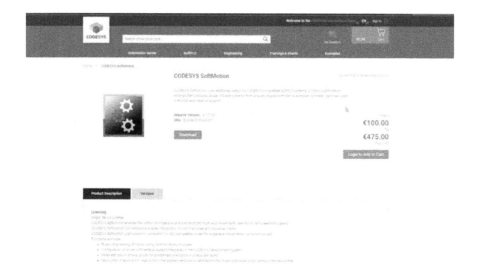

So what they need to do is click on download over here, because this will ask you for free your account or you will need to sign in. And once you have signed in, you can click again and download, you can agree on everything. And. After a while, you will have the package downloaded on your machine, and after a while you will have downloaded the adult package file. That you can simply double click. And after a while, it will open the code, says a package manager. And you can. Followed the installation process, read, understand and accept the license agreement. And. Here you can choose between a typical complete or customized setup. And we can use the complete set up. You can choose which installation of courses you want to use. And after that, too, you will need to wait for the package manager to install the package on your PC after a while, the installation will finish. You can click on next and then I'll finish.

ADDITIONAL LESSON HUNGARIAN NOTATION

We will talk about and giving notation and verbal naming conventions, then during notation is a naming convention which the name of the variable or a function indicates it's intentional type, meaning it is a set of rules. So there needs to be used when you decided the name of a variable or function. This is pretty useful because you would be able to tell something about the variable or function. Just looking at its name and anchoring notation is pretty popular in advance the policy programming. There are people that like using it and people that don't. And personally, I like using it, and in my opinion, it simplifies the life of a policy programmer. So in this course, Hungarian notation will be used. I will show you what kind of notation we will be using during the course. There are many types of annotations. This is just the one that I will use and the remember that using a consistent naming convention will simplify the definition and usage of of variables, especially in the scope in which many variables are defined and in PSC programming. This is pretty common. You may have a lot of variables in your P.O.S. application, and having a consistent naming convention will appear a lot. So this is the naming convention that I will use. You will have the variable name, as always. But other than that, I will add the two prefix to the variable one that will indicate the variable type and one that will indicate that the variable scope and this are the prefix for the variable type. So if you have a Boolean variable, you will add a next to the variable name before the variable name and I for an integer he who I saw insanely integer and so on.

Hungarian Notation - Naming Convention

Type Prefix

Prefix	Meaning
x	BOOL
i	INT
ui	UINT
di	DINT
r	REAL
lr	LREAL
tim	TIME
st	STRUCTURE
et	ENUM

These are pretty expletive on their own and will help you a lot when you are dealing with many variables. And this hour, the scope prefix, so will you will use no prefix if you are defining a local variable, you will use. I underscore for an input variable cue underscore for all the output variables, IQ for input variables and uppercase G for global variables. I KC for constant variables and the upper case and lower case C for global constant variables. All also prefix av an underscore after the letters. So let's look at some examples of variables definitions. So if I'm defining a variable called X product present on conveyor, this is a local Bohlen variable. It is local because it has no no scope prefix, and there's a bulletin variable because we have an X. If we have a new high number of products, this is a local unsigned integer. If we have a viable call, Underscore Star commented, This is a global variable and its type is a balloon variable. If we have a variable called IQ estimate or parameters, this is a 9lb structure. Again, another variable could be G C underscore L r convey your length, and this will be a global constant. Long, real, viable. This may seem a little strange for you if you have never used the Hungarian notations, but I assure you this will simplify your life when you will be dealing with bigger applications.

CREATE AN AXIS IN CODESYS

We will create our first motion control project in causes, and we will add our first axis to our project to. We will then look at the various configuration and parameters that will determine our axis behaviour. So let's create a new project that encodes this, and since we added a new package for the motion control using soft motion after we select a standard project. So let's call this motion control basic. After having added that, we will see that we have a new possible devices over here, and I suggested to choose the courses of motion when V3 existed before. If you have a 64 bit architecture or this one if you have a 32 bit. So I was like this and I will add the appeal you in the structural text language. So the main difference between a standard device and this one that we added in that we have the possibility to add the just because we have the soft motion package installed in code system is this soft motion general access pool that you see over here and within this one, we will be able to create access in our project. So let's see how to do that here. We can simply right click the access pool, click Add device, and over here you can see that we have a few choices and for what we need right now, we can create a virtual access. And the type is, as M underscore drive underscored, yet actual. Over here in name, we can't change it. And let's call this generic axis. And by clicking on Add device. You can see that we added a new object over here. Let's click on clothes and let's double click on the axis. And let's look at the different parameters that we have over here. In the general tab, we have a set of parameters that relate to the motion of the axis and its limits in the top left side, that we can configure the axis either as modulo axis or a finite axis.

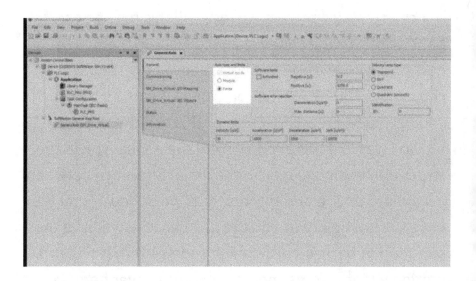

We will see this difference later in the course. But modulo axis are used to. Typically when you have an axis with a period like rotating axis while in steady use, finite axis four axis that don't have a period like linear axis. Then we have software limits that you can either activate or deactivate. That will limit the access position in a certain range. Then we have a software error reaction, meaning how the axis should behave when an emergency takes place, when an error takes place. So typically the axis should stop. And over here we specify the dynamic motion parameter for the emergency stop. On the right, we have a power to concerning the velocity ramp of the axis. We will see this later in the course, but this is about the acceleration and the celebration profile of the axis. And here we can choose between trapezoid since square, quadratic or quadratic smooth. There is quite a lot of documentation on the causes side and it could help and you can look on that. We have an identification part that is simply a unique I.D. for each axis. And on the bottom, we have some dynamic limits the limits for velocity, acceleration, deceleration and jerk for the axis. If you don't know, jerker is the derivative of the acceleration. Then we have the commissioning tab that is empty for us in virtual mode. So this should be specific to the manufacturer. So since we are using code this implementation for virtual access, we will skip this. Under the annual paying for the driver, we have only an option that is the bust cycle to. This means the cyclic task on which the target positions are passed to the driver. So over here we have only the main task right now. But typically, when you are working in the field of with field buses, you may have over here some tasks that are synchronous with the field buses. Then in the icy part, we can see that for the implementation of code system, the library creates an icy object for the object that we added in the policy configuration. So we can see that over here we will have a generic axis, a variable and it type is axis ref of your symmetry. And if we go in a, you know, we can try to write the generic axis, press control space and you can see that we have over here quite all of the properties and parameters. So since we are referring it to an icy object that is created alongside our PFC configuration object. Then over here, we have some status and some information regarding the object. Information is typically regarding the descriptor for the object. So over here we have some names of some vendor categories and so on. And for what concerns the status? Typically here we have some drive specific information that can be observed, the ones we are online regarding the status of the access and other things such as the communication and so on. So now let's get into simulation mode, and let's go online, even if we didn't write any line of code, we can see something regarding the axis when we are online. Since the view of the general tab changes, we can start the policy. And over here, we can see many different things when we are online. An online dashboard pops up on the left side. We have some information regarding the dynamic and kinematic variables of the axis. We have the set and the actual values of position, velocity, acceleration and torque. The difference between the set and actual value is that the set values are the ones that are requested by the policy, while the actual values are the one that are directly measured on the device.

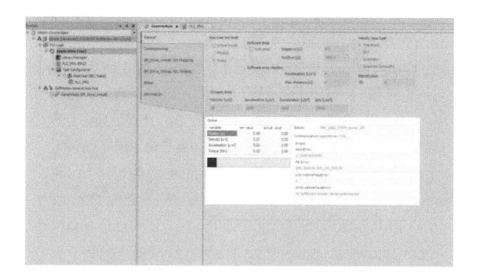

Since we are using virtual access, this two should match while in reality you would have the actual values trying to be the same as the set values, but they actually may differ a little bit, they will always differ a little bit. Then on the right side, we have a part concerning the status of the axis, meaning the operational status in which the axis is and as we can see right now, the axis is powered off. Then we have a part concerning the communication that for us is operational right now because we are using a virtual axis, but on real devices, you may find actual information about the communication. And then we have a narrow dashboard that will tell you if there is an error on the axis and what kind of error it is. And as you can see right now, we have no errors. We have a part concerning the axis error. So errors that are coming from the device and function block errors, so errors that are coming from a misuse of the motion control libraries. We have some additional information in the last string. And as you can see over here, we have a notice of motion license. So at the more modest has been started. But this is fine for us since we are in virtual mode. We will find some similar information on the status, so this tab. We'll also update when we are alone. And over here, we can see that right now our license is missing. So we are running in on mode. So right now, we haven't written any line of code.

INTRODUCTION TO THE SM3_BASIC LIBRARY

Before getting to the real programming, I just wanted to show you some details regarding the library for motion control courses. So when we create motion control, that project consists of motion, if we get to the library manager, we will find that over here, some libraries that are already related to motion control. You can see over here that we have a few libraries that are called. That is actually soft motion and we have one for basic motion control, one for C and C for robotics, robotics, visualization and transformations. Actually, in this course, we will only focus on the SM three basic and that's the library that we are going to use. That's the library that implements the PRC open standard. So if you just click on the SM three basic, you will find over here quite a lot of documentation regarding the function books. If you expand the same three basic folder and then the plus folder, you will get that all sorts of function blocks over here. Just one thing, the PRC opened function block. So the ones that are following the standard are called M.C. underscore something that stands for motion control. In this library, we have other blocks, other function blocks that are developed by courses at that they are not in the standard that are called that typically S.M. C or SM three.

And for instance, MSI Power is a function block that is in the standard and eSIMs C tree brake control. It is one that is not there, but the choice is that many manufacturers choose to develop some function book that may aid for their own implementation to carry out some additional features. And actually, we were mostly focus on function blocks that are in the PRC open standard that you should find on whatever motion controller you will use. And if you click on any function, look, you can see that over here, we have three tabs and input tabs that were an input output tabs that will show you all the inputs and outputs of the function block and also graphical overview. But mostly you will find the documentation and something regarding how the function book works. For instance, is related to a movement function. Look, I'm simple move absolute. You will find that quite all of the details regarding how they work and. This will be helpful when we will start using this function blocks. And whenever you have some doubts and you'll want to look up for some documentation, you can read the book online on. The courses are open, but it's good to know that you have quite a lot of documentation of over here. And in the library, you can find everything that's being used. You will find all the data types, so structures and the negatives, you will find the interfaces for the access and global variables that are declared when you have the library imported in your project. And you will also find some visualizations regarding the the all the functional blocks, and so typically these are frames that you can import in your Kurtz's visualization. You can link to any instance of the functional lo So if I said that I add them and seem overall relative in my project, I could have a visualization with an instance of this frame that I could link to the function block that is in the code part.

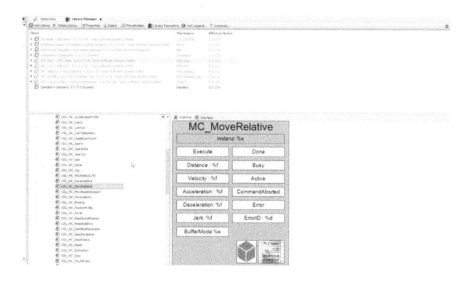

And I could directly use this in this buttons to change the the parameters and to interact with the axis. And this is something that is pretty useful, but for what I prefer, I typically like to have and. Implementation of the function book in FBD language in order to be able, let's say, to mess around with the function books. So Typekit. Typically, what I would do is to go in my in my program and I typically use a structured text. I would create an action. And I would use the FBD language, so let's call this motion control. That's because. I would go in the program and add some other call to this action. And over here, I would insert all the functional blocks that I need. So, for instance, if I were right over here and sea power. I would have the function book from the library.

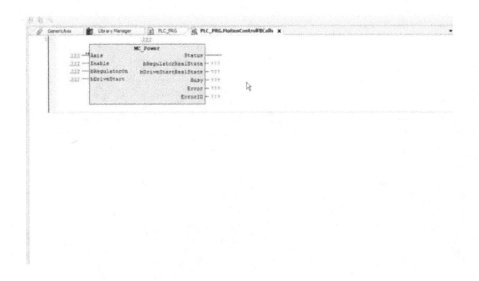

And of course, you need to create an instance of this, so this means nothing right now. But I just wanted to show you that what I typically like to do is ever this interface with all the inputs and outputs that are blank. And in this way, I can mess around and try out the function works. And this is pretty much the same of having this visualization implemented into your into your project. So this is what I will do for this course when we start to mess around and to try out the functional lo So bad, actually. You are free to do whatever you like. And this is only my view of things, but I actually like to use FBD for this, let's say, testing part. And once I started developing everything, I preferred to use only structured text.

HOW TO POWER ON AN AXIS (MC_POWER)

We saw diagnostics function blocks. And in this lesson, we will start to see how the power on access. So let's look back at our people see open state diagram and powering on an axis means to make a transition from the disabled state into the strength to state. So standstill means that the motor is power down and it is still it is not moving. And as you can see from the PRC on Penn State, diagram from the standstill state the motor can start moving and can get to any different emotional state. So let's see how to do that in code going to our library manager and getting to the same three basic peer use and to the administrative configuration of function books over here, we will find the MCP, our function book and the power function book is the one used to turn on the motor. So let's create an instance of this function, lo

So let's get into our CPG program, and let's add over here comments saying that this our diagnostic function blocks. And over here, we will have some administrative function blocks, and let's create a functional look that we will have the power and the type will be assigned three basic M.S. power. Let's get to our motion control function, Blackhall. And let's leave this on the bottom of the action. So let's add and talk about so right click over here in the second network and let's have the network here. Let's glass box here, and let's add the FBI power. Again, let's remove all the question marks. From. All the inputs and outputs are a function block and less at the axis input output over here generic axis. OK, so let's look at the interface. Over here, we have three inputs that are kind of much working toward the same goal. So the goal of this function block is to enable the axis to turn it on, and the first input enable is use that to enable the function lo So if we get to the documentation, you will see that enable will enable the execution of the function. So what this will do is make that function block operative. Then we have two different inputs that are used that, let's say, to definitely turn on the right one is used to enable the power of states. And one is just to disable the quick stop mechanism. So in order to turn on the motor, we need to have all three of these inputs equal to true one thing. And the first before that, we will see that the outputs are be regulatory on state. So this will be a feedback for the input and B drive real state that will be again a feedback for the second input and the motor will be turned on when the status becomes to. So actually, this outward status will tell you if the motor is powered on or not. Just one thing, and this implementation with these three variables is not actually the standard. This is mostly about could this because this does this in this century library, but in many other implementation, you may find and then see power function block that as only one input as the needle that would be was meaning would be. Let's turn on the access.

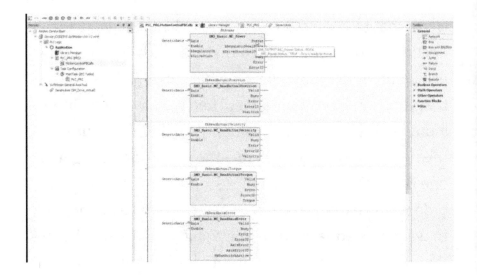

This input to only turns on the system and a status output. So typically the most standard implementation Julia has the enable and the status. No one ever regulated your own or right start or a regulator or real estate and start real estate. But let's see how this works. So we have placed this. Let's go online with a download. And let us start our application, and first of all, let's turn on the enable of the read status functional lo So as you can see, we are still in the disabled state. Less settled through the enable input of the power, as you can see, the status is still false and we are still in the disabled state. Lesser known or a greater Iran, as you can see, the regulatory state becomes through, but the status doesn't. And we are still. Right now, we are in this stopping state. This is because we have a quick stop operation over here running. So let's disable it and don't care too much about this because this is a standard operation for the PRC open so. If we have all three of these inputs equal to true, you can see that we get to this standstill operation to the standstill state. And, for instance, if I remove the enable over here. You can see that the stance still remains because we are still working. But if I remove this tube, we'll get into the disabled state again. So the SNC, the Surrey DMC power function block is what makes the transition from visible to stand still. And that if we just have the regulator on it at the start, we will get the stopping state. So this is how you power on your axis. And if you're going to the generic axis in the policy configuration, we will see over here again that the state is standstill. And once that function block, once the access is enabled, you can actually start moving it and you can do all the things that you want to do with it. But this is the preliminary stage and this is how you enable your power on your access.

RESET AN ERROR (MC_RESET)

We will see another function look, that is very important for the administration and the correct functioning of an axis. As you may know, whenever a machine is running or an axis is running, you may encounter some kind of alarm errors and unexpected behavior. So whenever something like that happens for any reason, you need the possibility, need to have the possibility to reset any alarm or error.

So looking at the PRC open state diagram, whenever an alarm is issued over the axis and counters in error, the axis will get into the errors stop state. When the axis is in the state, it needs to be reset in order to continue to work properly. So the transition from any state to the arrest of state is the fact that an alarm occurred then from the era stop. You can transition to the standstill state using the NC reset the function block. Unfortunately, we won't be able to simulate this because actually we do not have the possibility to generate hardware errors or errors regarding the physical stuff on the axis. But however, we can see how it should work. So let's get to our code and create a new functional lo Let's call this F.B. reset, and the type will be a simple three basic dot M.C reset. Let's go into our action to call the function look and just below the rest one, the power one, sorry. Let's add a new box. Let's call the f b reset. Again, here we can remove all the question marks and place our generic axis over here. So as you can see, this functional look is quite small. It has only one input and we have an execute input. So as I've shown you, exec means that this input is evaluated on the rising edge. So let's try to go online. We won't be able to do much, but let's see. If I enable the axis, let's also add the reed axis error and the read status. So right now, we are in a standstill state and if for some reason we got to the Earth's top state in order to move back to the standstill state, we would need to send and execute, come and do the F.B. reset.

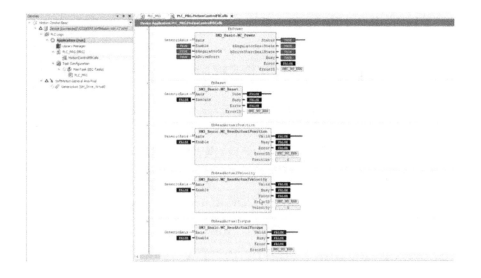

So if I did this, you can see that right now we get an error because here if I double click, it says no error to be reset. And over here in the status, we remain in standstill and we get this flag that tells us that an FBI error as occurred. And this is something new to the virtual state of our access, but we are not able to simulate an alarm that we can reset with the AMC récit. But in any case, this is very important for you. You should always have enough to be reached NMC resetting your code. And typically, if an alarm occurs so you should stop everything in your machine, you should display the alarm on some panel or some each mine and allow for a user to reset using a button. So you should that raise the execute of DSB reset when the real reset button is pressed. So this is very important, and you should always have an FBI reset in your code.

HOMING PROCEDURE (MC_HOME - SMC_HOMING)

So let's see how to carry out a numbing procedure in courses in order to do so, we will use the MSI home function block. First, let's look at the PRC open state diagram in order to carry out a norming. We need to get to the Omung State, so whenever we start aiming procedure from the standstill state, we will get into the homing state. Then when the mean procedure is terminated, we will get back to the stencil state. So let's see how we can do this in court this. First, we will need to create an instance of an embassy home, so let's create and be home, and the type would be assigned three basic north M.C home. Let's had a comment here, because technically the AMC Home is a movement function block. So in our playground program, we will separate them. So. Then let's get back in our action, and because of the great reset function, look, let's add a call to the FBI home and as we did for all our. Function blocks. Let's remove all the question marks and add over here a generic axis. So how does this work? We have an execute input that will start to the homing operation to its rising, and then when the operation is finished, we will get our done output. And here in the position input, we will set the value of the call that the axis will need to have won. The omega operation is finished.

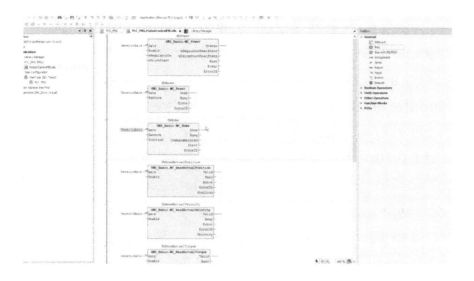

You can see that over here. We are not telling the axis what it should do for the women, so we are not asking for at the axis, you know, not asking the axis to look for a sensor in the positive direction, in a negative direction or something like that. And this is due to the fact that the same three basic is built in a way that it expects for all the homing parameters regarding the movement to be stored on the physical drive. So in some parameters, in some memory of the driver. So as you can see here, we have really minimal interface to do so. But actually here in the same three basic library, we have an actually an extended function block that is not part of the open standard that is called eSIMs C homing and that this is actually done. This is actually used to carry out and homing procedure with other more details that should be carried out within the bill, within the motion controller, not within the drive. We will see this as well. But actually, this is not part of the standard. So let's first take a look to our and see home function block. And since we are running a vertical axis and the omega operation will be instantaneous, so whenever we have a carry out an omega operation raising the execute, the position of the axis will be all written by disposition input. So let's try this, let's carry out the download. Let's start. And less power on the axis and with our sea power. And let us say that we were right hundreds here in our position and let's enable the grid status and the position function blocks. So we are right now in the stressful state and our position is zero. If I carry out an embassy bombing, pause the operation. Actually, I don't think we would be able to see it. But the state should move from standstill to bombing and back to standstill. And their positions should become on that. If I prepared the value and press comfortable life seven. Yeah, we didn't even see that that actually we got a done output for the B home and the position of the axis became a hundred. And we can see over here we also have 100. This does not mean that the is moved for 100. It means that it carried out homing procedure and at the end of the procedure, the Axis thinks that the position is

100 and this is quite straightforward when we are using virtual axis. But actually, for real axis, you will need to provide more information for the parameters and for the actual homing procedure that needs to be carried out.

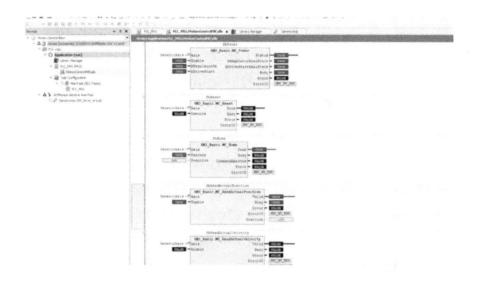

So let's take a look right now at that more complicated function block, just to get more insights on how it should work. So let's create another functional look that we will also that let's create another one that will be coming home extended and the Typekit would be a some three basic as emcee homing. And let's add a call over here. So right click and search network below, that's dragging a box over here, and that's too cold to be home extended. And as you can see over here, we have a lot more parameters. So let's remove again all the question marks for our function block. As you can see, the S and C function blocks use an Hungarian notation that in which B means Bowlin and F means flotsam. And these are real variables and so on. And this should be integer and this is different from the dentition I used about that. This is sent to, uh, confusing for you. So let's add here the axis, and let's take a look at the documentation for this function block. So again, we have an execute input that will start the operation, a very important parameter. Is this an alarming mode that is actually an enumerated? And these are different kinds of bombing procedures that can be carried out. So typically, this involves a fast and low velocity inversion once the the axis reaches a sensor. So. For instance, with Mod Zero, the axis will move with a faster velocity. To look for for a reference which then it will invert its direction and move out of the reference rates so it will wait for it, will move fast once must wait for the reference switch to become true. It will change direction and move with a low velocity until the reference it becomes false. And then it will set the position to the value that we request and then stop. Then over here, we have some other other possibility in which first it will stop and then we'll execute the set position. So the difference is that it will wait to stop before setting the position, and therefore it will be less precise on the actual position in which the reference fits the reference, which changed the value.

And we have other modes that will involve an index falls on the Inquisitor. But we will not look into those and we have this other two in which the weights the motor won't invert the direction, so it will move in a direction, get true value for the reference reach and move. Keep it moving with a slower velocity in the same direction and wait for the reference switch to become false. And. We can simulate this and there, and the important thing about this function block is that the reference feature will will come from the PRC. So you can see over here we have a bee reference region that will be the actual value for the reference feature that should be theoretically linked to a physical input on the PRC, as you can see in the MCU. We didn't have that because it was expected for the home for the reference speech that to be directly wired on the drive. So typically an approach like this is a little bit slower because actually you have a field bus communication between the reference, which ended, right? Well, instead of having the reference suites directly via the on the drive will lead to a faster response on the motor. But actually, both of these possibilities are quite used and quite viable in the market. So getting back to our documentation on the same sea homing, sorry, here you can see the outer perimeter, so we have the composition that is the same of the position for the home. So for them, see homeless. So the position that will be set when the when the actual when the homing procedure is terminated, we have this velocities low and velocity fast that will be used some acceleration and deceleration parameter. These are motion parameters for the movement that will take place. We have a new parameter that you can live to zero if you don't want to use jerk, but this actually is the the derivative of the acceleration and is the actually the unit of measurement is unito versus the cubic. Then we have some other parameters regarding the delay for the reference which to be transmitted, and we have a bit that can be used to move the motor back to a zero position when the homing is finished and other things. That are typical enough to use the for instance, if you want to ignore the Outer Limits and other configuration for the axis.

But actually, let's try this. So let's go online and with a download. Let's start here, we have a reference switch to the truth. And this is due to the fact that this many homing pursuit omega sensors are typically normally closed sensor, so this means that the true means that the limit switch is open. You can see that why we hover this, but so through means that the switch is open and force means that the switch is closed. So we need to when we treat the switch, we will have this getting to false. So let's try this, for instance. So let's enable our access, let's enable our read actor position and read status. And. Let's write some parameters for this. So let's say that we want to move in a negative direction. This is fine for us that when we get there, we get to the limits which we want to zero on the axis. I say that this low velocity should be, I say, one unit per second and the first velocity should be 10 units per second. And as acceleration, let's add 100 units per second squared. This means that we will get to the next to the velocity faster in one tenth of a second and to the velocity was low in one hundredths of a second. Let's not use a jerk and that is any delay. And let's select one of these homing mode. So let's get back to how our homing mode. And we could use it as fast stop and fast slow stop, so we won't change the direction of the movement or once we get the sensor. So we will move in a negative direction with a fast velocity. And get the sensor over with a slow velocity in the same direction and then set the position and stop. And let's also read the actual velocity over here. OK, so we are enabled, we can start. As you can see, the position of the axis is moving backward with a velocity of minus 10 because this is the fast velocity and we can see it as well in the generic axis. So let's simulate our reference tweets. So if I send this to force, it should start moving with a slower velocity and then wait for the sensor to disappear. So actually, it inverted the velocity. Let me see what I chose. I chose this fast because low a stop. OK, sorry, I chose the one that inverts, so it inverted the velocity. So right now, it's moving in a positive direction. And once I reset the reference region, what I should, we should see the position becoming zero after it stop. So as you can see, it is not zero because in this homing operation, it said the value before here, let me see which one I'm using. So we have the be little stop. So sorry, is this one? And as you can see, it will set the position in the stock. So actually, we have a small distance that is that we will actually run across before stopping and let us get deeper into this by creating a trace. So if you don't remember what the Tracy is, it's a simple way to show some variables changing in time. So here I will create a trace. The trait, the task I will choose is the main task. I can do this while online, and let's add some variables for the trace. So here I can click on the configuration at variable. So the first variable I will trace is will be CPG Dot, FBI read actual position. That position? The second one will be to underscore PIRG Ashby reactor velocity, not velocity. And I will add the PRC underscored PIRG that had be home and extended, not sorry, not that axis backed up the reference switch. OK, then also let's go into the trees and go into the advance. And as you can see, we're here. We have 40 seconds of recorded samples and let's add a zero over here to six minutes and in order to avoid for the buffer to get the buffer emptying as we show the trees. So let's right click over here and select to move all variables to individual dry diagrams. And let's download Trace. OK, so as you can see here, we have the reference which equal to one. And because it is not trick and the axis is not moving because the velocity zero and the position is that zero point zero zero five. So let's drag this window over here. And have two different windows for this. Sorry. I will download

again. And let's do this again. So I will set back the
execute the force and I will set it to true again. OK, so we
can see that the position start decreasing, we are moving
backwards. When the reference, which is three. We will
start moving forward at a slower velocity, and once the
switch is not tripped again, as you can see, the position is
now zero. But it doesn't mean that the axis move from
this position to this instantaneously, it simply changed the
whole meaning of the axis. So for the axis, this position
that we had here is zero. So let's stop the trace. And as
you can see, if we Zoom, you can see that the change in
the set position, so the position is set to zero before the
axis stopped. And this is due to the homing method that
we chose. So according to the type of machine that you
have through your architecture and the to the mechanics,
to how it is assembled, you should actually choose the
homing method and the homing parameters accordingly.
So this is not part of the PRC open standard. And typically,
if we use this MQM, you should have some kind of
parameters, something like this that should be written
and downloaded onto the drive physically. And yeah, this
is it for the homing procedure.

SETPOSITION PROCEDURE (MC_SETPOSITION)

We will see an another way to reference an axis that is called a set position. This is done through the AMC set position function block that is actually an administrative function block. So we will in society here. So over here, all right. F be set position. The type would be a SIM three basic AMC set position. And if we're going to the library manager and the administrative function blocks, we will find it here, and this functional look is used to set the position of the axis without actually moving it.

So in this way, we will be able to shift the coordinate system of the axis. So this is something like what happens when you carry out a norming procedure, and the main difference is that you don't move the axis. You don't look for a sentence, sir, and you simply shift the reference the coding system for your axis. So we will try it right now and we will see how it works. So that add a call for this function work. Yeah, that's placing it under the home extended. So right click Insert Network below through our guide box. And this will be our FDA set position. Let's copy the axis in the into the axis input output. And as always, let's remove all the question marks. OK, so over here we have a version, but we have the execute as always, with the position that we want to use for our set position operation and a mode input, a mode that is a bolt on variable. And we can see better in the documentation that this is used to carry out either a relative set position or a absolute position. And we will just see the difference between these two. So let's go online and let's mess around with this function. Lo Let's start off, you'll see. And. That enable the access. And let's. Enable our civil status and most importantly, our emcee. Read actual position. So right now, the position of our axis is zero. And if I call I, if I execute our set position function, look, let's say with a position of 100 units.

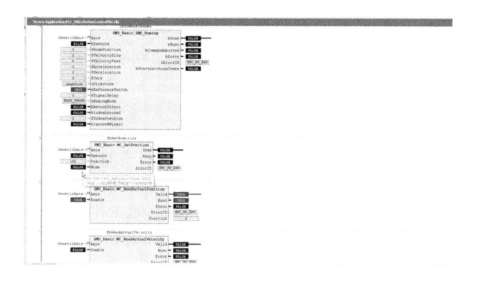

And with an absolute mode, so more needs to be false. If I carry out and execute. I get it done over here, and you can see that the position of the axis is now 100th. So this means that it simply changed the position of the axis. It didn't move. The very important thing to understand is that it did the move and this when we are in a virtual environment, this may seem very similar to a norming that actually they work in a different way. So when you carry out the norming in virtual mode, this is actually a set position. But with the real axis, you will actually you would actually see a movement and look for a sensor. Instead, the set position was simply changed the accordion system for the axis. So as far as you can see, I wrote hundreds, let's do that again with two hundred. And this is how it works for the absolute moment, the absolute model is simply override to the position of the axis with the one that you that you have over a year. And instead, if we won, we use the relative mode. What would happen is is that the position that we were right over here will be added to the current position. So if you carry out a relative position with two hundred and I'm a 200 right now, carry out and execute. You can see that the position has become 400. So the set position in the relative we will actually carry out the correction will carry out a position setting in an incremental way or in the relative way. So in the PRC open standard, you will find it in different and in different scenarios, the relative and absolute word. So. Whenever you talk about the absolutist position or absolute movement, you need to think that you are thinking of the position as an absolute value. So 200 means that the target will be 200 instead if you're using the relative mode. 200 is added to the current one and we will see this later on when we talk about this quick movement. And let's talk a little bit about why we need dysfunction block and when it is used, you will use this function block when you need to change the reference the cooling system of your axis, not because you are doing, you know, Mumbai, but maybe because you need the you need it for external ways. So maybe when you get an external sensor, you will need it to start again and this will need to be your zero the zero of your most of your axis. Or this is actually used a lot when you are dealing with virtual axis, and you will also be dealing with beautiful X on the real machine because they are useful for synchronization and synchronized movement. And this is actually quite useful and allows you to do quite a little bit. They say a lot of tricks and you will be able to manipulate the position of your axis according to external factors that are not the homing sensors.

MOTION SETUP

Before we start to talk about movements and before we start using you, you'll see open function blocks for movements. Let's first set up a phrase that we will use throughout the movement lessons. So we had this trace over here, but let's delete this and let's right click an application and object trace. And let's link it to the main task. And let's call it the three generic axis. So we're here. Let's get into the configuration, and let's add three variables. The first one will be the position of the axis and the first simplicity, now let's just simply look at the axis that we have in policy configuration. So I will write the generic axis that f act position. This will show the actual position of the axis. The same one that we would read using the right exact position function block. Then the second variables should be generic axis, not affect velocity. That is actually the same as the reactor velocity function block. And over here, let's set up a generic axis that affect acceleration. So in this way, we will keep track of the position if the derivative is secondary. So in this way, we would be able to track down what is happening.

When we move an axis. Let's click OK, let's move them all to individual diagrams. And again, let's go into configuration advanced. And over here, let's add a zero to have enough buffer that is big enough for four of samples.

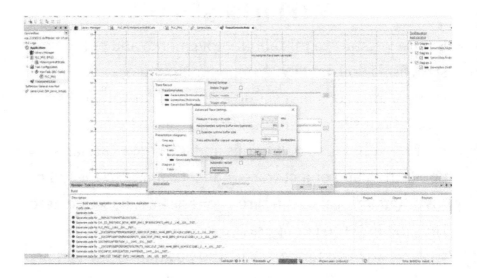

So right now we are set up and we will start to talk about movements in the next next lessons. And also, let's make some order in our faction blocks, call action. So let's add a network above the first one. So let's divide. What are we calling? What are we calling diagnostics a function? Lots more social function blogs and so on. So this will be administrative. So I added a network over here and I will toggle the command comment state. And I will right click and insert the label, so in this way, you will come and come over here and say administrative function blocks. And also, let's move the set position above, so I will control access and control. So we have these three administrative function blocks. Over your glasses, certainly not sorry. As first ad network below. And you're saying that these are the motion function blocks because by the standard that we will have the movement function blocks over here, we in the same ceiling. So here, let's again toggle the comment label. Let's see this movement function blocks. And then after this. And that would blow cargo come later, come and state. And this was will be diagnostic function. So in this way, we have made some order about what we have in our action. So the next lesson we will see the movement wants and we will have them below here below this extended.

INTRODUCTION TO CONTINUOUS MOTION

We will start to talk about the continuous motion. Continuous motion is one of the three motions that can be achieved in the open, and it is about moving an axis with some movement that can persist in time. Meaning that if it is not stopped, that it will go on indefinitely, at least theoretically, and it is not about movements that have a certain start to. Instant and that and instant, they can go on in perpetuity.

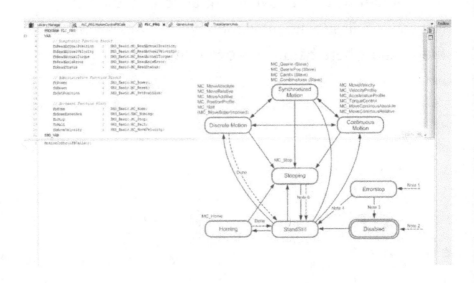

So looking at the state diagram, you can see that from the standstill state, you can go into a continuous motion state and this will be achieved within execute rising trigger of the function block that is used for the movement. And as you can see, there is no direct transition back to a distance to state. You can go to the Stancil state using stop using and then see Stop. You will get to stopping or and then to standstill. Or alternatively, you can always use and see hold. You will get into the discrete motion and then back into the standstill when that done, output gets equal to true. we will look at continuous motion function blocks and we will see how they work.

STOP AN AXIS (MC_STOP & MC_HALT)

Before we start to move axis to and to carry out movements, we will need to know how we can stop the movement of an axis. This is a very important topic. It is very important also for safety reasons, and I will show you what are the main differences between the safe, controlled stop the and the stop that is not safely controlled, so. The Bielski open standard, there are two main function blocks that can be used to stop and access this function blocks are the AMC hold and the AMC stop. So let's create them, let's instantiate them and call them, and then I will show you, what are the main differences between this function? So let's create an SB stop. The type will be a simple three basic dot AMC stop and and behold. The type will be a simple three basic dot AMC hold.

Let's go into the motion control function because. And let's not call for this function looks so. Oh, over. Sorry. Over here. That's in certain network. New box. And that's called the FBI stop. New network below. New box, and let's call the FBI hold. OK, let's copy the axis on both function blocks and remove all the question marks. And. As you can see. This function blocks look rather similar. One could almost say that they are the same as their interface. There is one important difference both in behavior and in interface. And as you can see, the only difference is that the MSI staff doesn't have the command, the bolted output, and there is a reason for that. So let's talk about what happens when you use one of these. So you have yet to input on this at the celebration that will specify what is the the celebration that you needed to stop your access. And the jerk from that again, is the derivative of the acceleration and will determine how smooth is the deceleration curve. And this is important for the stop. But if you place zero over here, you want use, you will use the maximum jerk, so you will have a step in the situation.

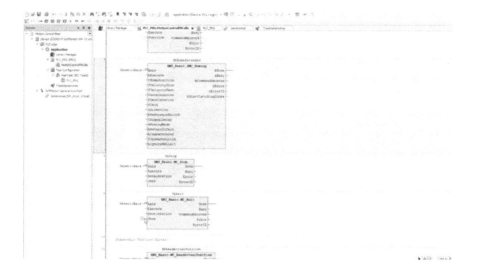

So from outside, you will actually see that if you raise the ticket of either of these function blocks while you're moving, the axis will stop and everything will seem the same. But actually, they are quite different. So. Let's also look at our possible state diagram. Let's first talk about what happens if we use NMC hold the M.S. that is actually intended as a discrete movement functional lo So that discrete movement function is our function books that start a movement that will and and will eventually end. So for this function, look, the movement is the stopping procedure. So you will raise the execute the your axis, who will transition to that this quick movement state, and once it has finished, it will get back to the standstill state.

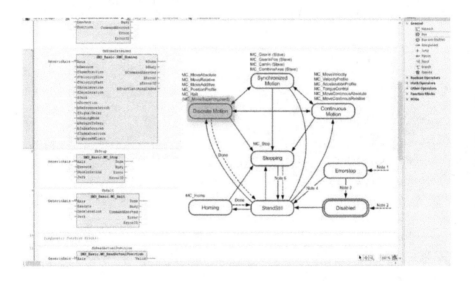

An important thing is that any discrete movement can be aborted and can be stopped, can be preempted by any other functional lo So for instance, if I am carrying out an hold and I want to use another function block to carry out the movement, it will simply it will simply interrupt the the separation ramp and it will start to the new movement. So this feature makes the whole procedure, let's say, not so safe way to stop the access. If you want to still stop the access in a safer way, you will need to use the AMC stock. So if you risk the execute the embassy, stop the access will start to try to decelerate again in the same way. But it won't transition to the this to the discrete movement state. It will transition to the stopping state and as you can see, you can transition to the state from anyone. And when you are there, you will be allowed to leave the state. Only if you stop being as finished and if you if you set the execute input of the stop to force, if you don't do this, you won't be able to get out of the stopping state. And the most important thing is that you won't be able to command any other movement. This is because the stop is the locking function block, and it is important that it will lock the access and it won't allow you to do anything unless the access is stopped. So let's go online and see this. So let's carry that download. I already did that. So I will read that worm. So let's go to our power function, block and enable the access. And let's also enable the read status. So we will see what is the status of the access versus status right now. And I will set the deceleration input of both function blocks, let's say, 200. I need to do that because if I leave the room, I will get the function block error. So what happens if I? Use the AMC host. I will press seven the way we look at the status, but actually we won't see any transition to the discrete motion because it is too fast. We are already in the Stancil state. We have did just this constant velocity flag that means constant velocity equal to zero. So we are still but actually I could have preempted this hold in any time. Instead, if I use this stop, so I our press control of seven, now you can see that right now I'm in stopping state. We are in the stopping state. And unless I set the execute input to force, we will still be in the stopping state. So here I remove the execute and we're back into standstill. As you can see, you are allowed to stop even if you are still, you don't get an arrow. And now if I get the message, stop running. So I have the exact equals the. We are in the stopping state. And if I try to command and hold, that is actually a discrete motion function block birth control of seven. You can see that I have I will receive a command aborted command aborted because I won't be able to do anything unless they release the stop. So if I remove this. I remove this. I carry out an act now I'm able to. So this is the very important difference between the FBI staff, sorry, AMC Stop and the AMC halt. And in my experience, the AMC stop is much better. I if you have some doubt about which one to use, I suggest you. My personal opinion is that you should use the AMC stock because you are much safer and you can control better your the safety of your access.

CONTINUOUS MOTION - VELOCITY PROFILE (MC_MOVEVELOCITY)

We will start to move our axis and we will take a look at the main continuous motion function block of the PRC open standard. That is the AMC move velocity function. Like this function block is used to cause an endless motion at the specified velocity. So using this function block, we will be able to start moving an axis in that direction at the specified velocity. So let's first instantiate the function block. So let's go over here and create an FBI move velocity. The type will be a simple three basic dot AMC move velocity. And let's go into our action. And in the move and function block, let's add a new network and the new call to the function block. So as we always do and you box have been move velocity. Let's remove all the question marks. And let's add our access, our generic axis to the axis input. OK, so let's comment a little bit. What are the important outputs of this function look and how it works? So as you can see, this is an exact function block. So this means that the function block will start on the rising edge of the execute input. You can see that over here you have a specified value of velocity that is in the main parameter for this function block, we have acceleration, deceleration and jerk for the transition. So if your axis starts is in a standstill phase and you will, you want to move, start moving it at a specified velocity. It will transition to that velocity using the parameters that you specify over here then. Here we have a direction input that, as we can see in the documentation, the type is in, then see direction that is not a function block. This is not a function block.

This is simply an an inauguration. So over here we have many different type of direction. But for this kind of function, look for that move velocity. The only one that matters are the positive and negative. So. If I wanted to move it forward in a positive direction, I would write AMC direction that positive or if I wanted to move it backward, I will write and see direction that negative. You can always also use the values that are specified over here so you could use one or minus one. The other ones are mainly for the discrete movement function blocks this that we will discuss later in the course. So and also, sorry, we have this buffer mode that is not actually often used, but some implementation of the standard, this buffer mode and the buffer mode, as you can see. Sorry. As you can see here. The finance, the chronological sequence of the function block relative to the previous block. So. In the past few months, the function look standard, typically the normal way of working is that if a function book is using an axis and another function block starts, so it receives an executable through the first one will abort. And this is the typical way of working for open function works by some implementation of this buffer. Mody input that is actually about a different way of working for this, let's see, kind of sequence. So. Typically, you will abort the function block if another one is started, but in other cases, you may want to buffer different movements or also create a blending within this movement. This is not often used, but it's nice to know that it is here. But anyway, this isn't the main topic of this lesson. So we have a dysfunction block. And let's also look at the outputs. As you can see, we have an execute function block, but we do not have it done. We have a nine velocity, and this output is equal to true once the velocity has been reached. So let's go online and try to make it work and understand how it works.

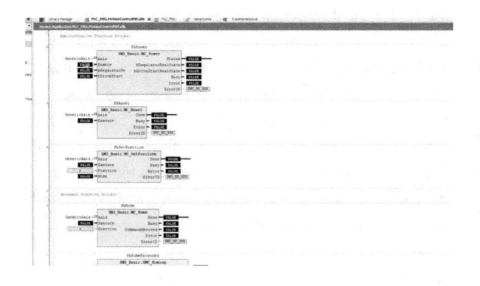

So. We have started everything, so let's turn on our axis. And let's also set to say the actual actual position and actual velocity and also the lead status that's enabled them. And let's open our trace that we had from the previous lesson. That's right click and download. So. Right now we are seeing the position, the velocity index and acceleration of our axis, oh, sorry, this is inverted. So this is the position. This is the velocity and this is the acceleration for me. So. Let's try to place some parameters over here. So let's choose a positive direction. So double click that, select the positive. And let's say that we want our access to reach at velocity of our units per second. Let's say that we want to accelerate with an acceleration of 50 units per second square, and let's say that we will have this operation that is half of that. So 25 units per second square. So what should happen right now when we start this function? Look, we'll be executing. We will first need to get to the velocity. So the velocity will have a ramp. And since we are accelerating at 50 unit per second per second, it should take two seconds to reach the velocity that we specified. So and after that, it will mean it will continue with that philosophy and in the acceleration, we will only see acceleration and at none zero acceleration in the first part. When the function book starts, then the velocity will be constant and the position will be increasing at a constant rate. So let's see what happens. You look at the position, we can see that the position is increasing. So the axis is moving. We can see that the velocity is constant. So the position is increasing at the constant rate and that this can also be seen by the fact that over here we have zero acceleration. But what happened in the transition militarization? We had a two second acceleration and we can see it over here. Would that an acceleration that was exactly 50 seconds squared? And this is the position so we can see here that at the beginning, the velocity was zero and it slowly increased with a trapezoid at trapezoidal profile. So this is nice, we can see it working and. The axis is moving. This is a linear axis, so you can see that the position is always increasing. Now let's remove the execute. And also, we can see that the velocity is through. That's one of the execute, and let's say that we want to go to negative 100 units per second. So we need to maintain this equal to 100 and simply change. The direction. So what will happen? We will start. Decelerating so the velocity will will become smaller and smaller with the deceleration chute, so you would take around four seconds to get to zero. Then it will get negative. With a rate of change that is given by the acceleration, so the deceleration is you the one we are transitioning from a higher velocity to a lower velocity. And we are speaking in absolute value. Instead, the acceleration is is that when we are transitioning from lower velocity to a higher velocity. So let's try. Execute equal to true. OK, so this is not very easy to see, but you will see that. Here in this transition. We were using a 25 minus 25 acceleration, so we were decelerating. And you can see that this ramp is less and less steep than this one. So. Once we got to a zero velocity, we can use a cursor here to see the values. Once we got to a zero velocity over here. Sorry, here was around zero. Then the acceleration. Raised so we started changing to change our velocity in a much faster way. So as you can see, this portion took us for a second and this portion took us two seconds. And right now, we are moving backwards, so we are going from. We are moving in a negative direction. So along decreasing positions. And we can see the position here is decreasing, the velocity is minus hundred, so and in a negative direction. And let's say that we want it to or sorry, we are also in the continuous motion state. And we are constant velocity, and you would see also these values in the transition, so acceleration thing or decelerating according to what we are doing. And let's say that we want to stop. If we want to stop, let's say that we want to make a very strong stop, so like an emergency stop, so we have a 500 units per second squared deceleration. And we will use this stop control and if seven. We can see that we use this very strong deceleration, and we stopped, so velocity one to zero position stop and remain at the customs value that is the one, the one in which we were when we commanded the stop. I mean, after the transition to stop. So we have small delay given by the fact that we need some time to stop. So let's say we received the common when position was in this my case and seventeen hundred and seven, and we stopped around that. Sixteen hundred and ninety four.

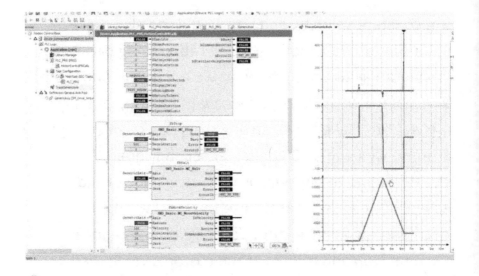

So this is how it works with the stop and the move velocity. And as you can see here, the velocity received, did this come under aborted? Why? Because it was using the axis, it was controlling the axis and someone aborted his command. And it was this top. So we were aborted. And if this gets through all the output, we'll get to sorry, this gets to falls or the output will get false. So the comment about it is is reset. And right now we are in the stopping state. So if we want to start a new movement. You can see that we are not able to we will get an error. It is. Ax is not ready for motion. And if we remove these top execute, we will be then able to move again. So this is was that what's happening? Let's fly with the Hulk so you can see the difference. So right now, if I use the Hulk. You can see that we have the dance and the commander bolted on the move velocity as before, but actually I can start a new movement. Without resetting the hold. And let's also try in a different way. So let's try to stop that with a very small deceleration. So let's say 10 units per second square. This means it would take 10 seconds to stop. And here. If I do that, you can see that we are decelerating. But if I start a new movie velocity. You can see that this this kind of stop was aborted by the move velocity. So this is the main difference between the stop and the hold, the Stacpoole will never be aborted. If you use an embassy stop, you will always stop, but the old can be aborted. And yeah, this is our and AMC movie Velocity works, and we are now using a linear axis so you can see that the position is always can increase or decrease with our limits. And in the next lesson, we will take a look at the differences between art and linear axis and modulo axis for what concerns the move velocity. We will also see some differences when we will be talking about discrete movement.

CONTINUOUS MOTION - FINITE VS MODULO AXIS

We will take a look at the difference between a finite axis and the modular axis for what concerns continuous motion. So. We saw that with leaner axis. We will get the ever increasing position or ever decreasing position in a negative way as well. So actually for Funny Texas, you have a final or leaner axis, you will have a position that will always be continues. So we will not have any discontinuity on the position unless you carry out an comingle or set position. And let's first look at the feature of a finite axis. And I mean, this is something that you also may find on the modular axis, but typically you will only use this in finite taxes. So here? These are the softer limits. So with this. They will be able to activate the software limits of an access. And over here you can specify what are the negative limit and the positive limit. Of course, the positive limit must be bigger than the negative one. So what will happen if the motor if the access gets to one of these two limits, it will carry out an emergency stop and you will get two to the arrows top state in the PRC open state diagram. So let's see it. We will need to carry out a download. And let's start our program. Let's carry out a download for the Trace.

So it starts, and let's see. That's turned on the axis and turned on the red states. Then let's commander, move velocity. Let's see what the velocity of 400, acceleration of 400 and deceleration of 400. OK, so we are moving toward the positive, softer limits. We can't see 800 1000. Yes, we stopped. You can see that we had the celebration here with the minus 1000 in the square and our axis to the. And you can see that this value has been taken from this dynamic limits and. Because we didn't specify and all of the celebration for software, but right now we are in the House state. Ever stop state of the PRC open state diagram, so in order to get out of it, we will need.

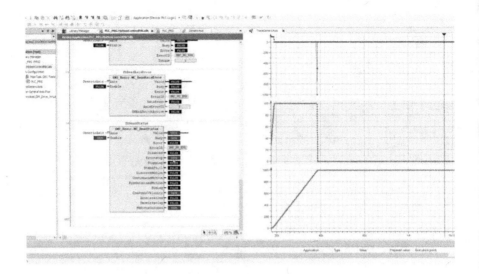

One thing that you will also see her over here and in order to get out of the state, we will need to give and next Typekit arising adds to this récit function bo So we got her down here, and you can see that we are back into the stands to face sensitive state. And let's try to move again forward. And you can see that we try to move just for a fraction of a unit, so we are still below one thousand and we are back into the other state. So whenever you get to South Korea limits, you're not able to move further in that direction. So if I reset and let's say that we move back. So get back to the more velocity and selective and negative direction. Control and F7 and. Download the trace again. And as you can see right now, this is allowed the access is moving back and we are in continuous motion state of the art. Eventually, we will get to zero. That is the negative limit. And we get to the Arrow stuff again. So this is how the software limits feature work. Now let's get back offline, and let's see how the modular axis works. And as I told you, model access means that the axis is periodic. So there is a period to the axis. And typically this is done for a rotating axis. So it doesn't matter if you are, let's say, a zero degree or a 360, 720 and so on. Because the absolute position will actually be the same for you. It doesn't form. It doesn't really mean anything to be at zero to sixty seven, twenty one thousand eighty and so on. Because for you, your axis is periodic. So let's create an axis with a model of 360 and let's go online. We can see that over here. We have a different graphics for the axis, and let's try to see what happens when we start moving. So again, let's get back to our. Function looks.

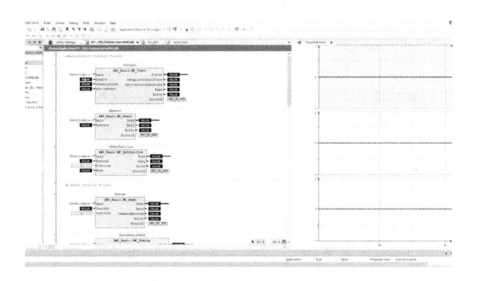

And sea power turned on that's also turned on the reduction of velocity and position which status. And, uh. And let's again, move forward, let's see with the velocity and acceleration of 110 deceleration of 100. Excuse. Let's look at the position. This is what happens. You can see that the position. Remains into the range between zero and 360. This is called the rollover, so the access will do a rollover in order to remain in that range. But as you can see, the axis is still moving forward is that we do not see any difference in the velocity and the acceleration. And this is simply a logical way to look at the position of an axis and that the actual benefit of doing something like that will become really clear when we look at discrete movement function blocks. But this is actually very important for the configuration of an axis. So in this way, you will see that the position is always in this range. And actually, we get back to zero every 360 degrees. So this is very important and this is the only difference between linear axis and relative axis. And one suggestion on my side is death. If you want if you for your needs, for your application, if you have an axis that will need to operate in continuous motion, always in the same direction. My suggestion is to use rotating axis, so a model axis. And this is important because in this way, your position will be contained in a certain range and you will not have drift in position that even if we are using long real after a while, you may have precision issues. So or if the a real axis or if the real drive and those to the position as an integer. So let's say a double integer or a long integer, you will have a rollover issue. So. My take on this and my suggestion for you is that you will need all of Iraq's need model access for access that always go in in the same direction.

MANUAL CONTINUOUS MOVEMENT (MC_JOG)

We will talk about another function block that is used for the continuous motion of analysis. Dysfunctional is the AMC jargon that is used for the jogging of an axis. So jogging meals to command the motion of an axis at a constant velocity, typically with a push and all that type of a button or switch. So jogging is typically used for manual motor control, meaning that if you want to manually move a motor from one position to another using a button or switch, you will typically use a jug feature or functionality. And the for the P.O.S. Open Standard, you will find out the M.S. Jog Function Lock. So let's take a look at it just in our library here in the movement. You will find the AMC jog. And let's create it, and let's create an instance of it, and let's try it out. So let's call it FBI Jog and the Typekit Zamzam three basic data M.S. JAG. And as always, let's get back to our social function, lo New network, new box, sorry. Created two networks New Box.

And he will have an FBI job. That's faced the axis and remove all the question marks and then let's talk about how the function block interface is. So here you may see that this works is quite similar to the move velocity.

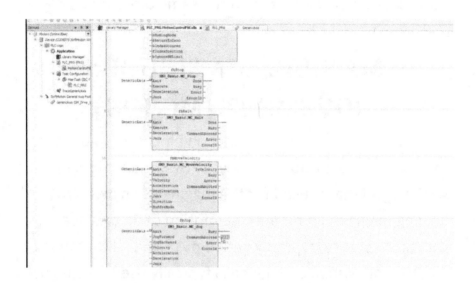

You will find the velocity acceleration solution and jerk for the movement. And this is quite similar because both of this function blocks command a constant velocity movement for the axis. And you can see that over here we have two inputs that are jog forward and backward. This are the inputs. And actually, they work, let's say, in an enabled fashion. So this are typically linked to physical buttons that are push and hold Typekit. So they will be true only if the button is pushed. Otherwise, they will be false. So typically, if you set it to set the joke forward through the axis will start moving forward. And once you set it back to force, the axis will stop. And the same will occur for jumping backward, but of course, moving backward. So one thing before starting up, let's set our eye on axis to fine it with the activated software limits in case you add the modular axis in here, and let's get back online to try this out. So let's carry out a download, let's start the PRC. And as always, less turn on the power. And let's get also into the rich status, and let's turn it on. Let's also open the trace. Put it right here on the right. Right click Download Trace. OK, so let's see what happens. First of all, let's put some parameters over here. So again, Velocity 100. And let's also use 100 as acceleration deceleration. And let's not use the jerk. So chug forward. It will see that we access this one over here. The red one is the position is moving forward. If I remove the joke forward, you can see that it stops within the dynamic parameters that we inserted as acceleration, deceleration and jerk. The same way, if I move backward. It will keep moving backward until I remove them, but. So this is mainly how it works, and it is similar to the move velocity, and you will see that if I jog the state, the policy open state will become continuous motion. So and this way is pretty similar. And the main difference is that if you remove the input, it will stop, so it will get back to the stance the state. And again, if I try to send, let's say, a stop, so I will use 100 units per second squared deceleration.

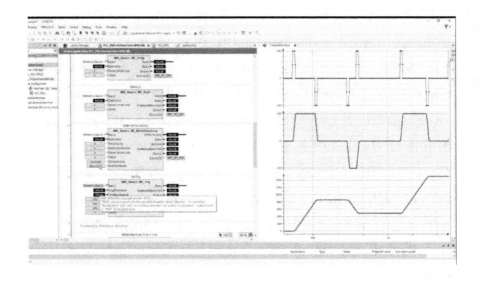

And if I stop, it will stop. And he will see that the judge
again is an observer to both function block so can be
aborted just as any other. So the main thing here is that
why should you in what let's say, in what conditions
should you use a jog or move velocity? So the jog should
be used the one you are dealing with manual control or
manual movement. So as I said, but linking the inputs of
the jog function block to some type of switches or
buttons. More velocity instead should be used when it is
crucial to the machine operation. So typically in an
automatic mode, not in a manual one. So. The move
velocity will start some job and it will keep work, keep
going until you either use a stop or not, when the jog can
be stopped by disabling the button. So this function

mainly exists only for the manual type of operation. And you should use this only for that purpose. You could achieve the same behavior of an embassy jog with a combination of a move velocity and a stop, but actually you don't need to. It works quite fine in this way. And you will have the same kind of functionality, but remember quite important to move velocity for automatic purpose, jog only for manual purposes.

PROJECT 1 - FAN MOTION – INTRODUCTION

We will take a look at the first project of this course, so please download the attached the resources and you will find that project file. And you can try to open. And in case you have some difficulties, some technical difficulties opening the last project file, you can open the doThe Project Archive file. So once you open the project, you will find something like this. So I will walk you through everything that you have in the project and what you need to do for this exercise. So first of all, we have a visualization. This exercise is about controlling AFM, and we will do so using the concepts that we learned for the continuous motion operation of PRC open function blocks. So you will find a visualization that you will use to interact with your machine. Your This visualization is equipped with a lot of buttons on the right side and some feedbacks on the left side. You will be able to to interact between the aura within this HMRC and your program using a set of global variable list. Here you have a set of comments that are variables that come from the HMRC and feedbacks, so something that you need to write as feedbacks for the user on the page may indicate you made. All of these are buttons and all of these are feedbacks. Then we have some parameters over here that will be used in your program will need to be used in your program as study parameters. And I know in some real applications they could be modified, but for now we can think them as fixed parameters. So let's talk about how this works and what are the specifics of this project. So the idea is that we are controlling your phone, we're controlling your phone, and we have two modes for operation of our farm. We have a manual mode or an automatic mode in the manual mode.

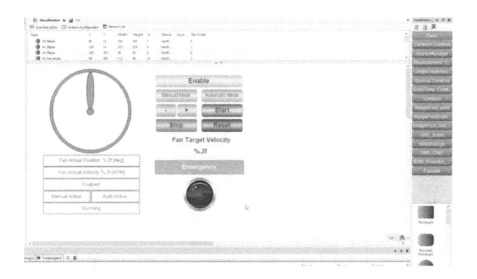

We can mostly do a jog operation, so pressing the plus or minus we can move forward or backward, or we can move our friend forward or backward instead in the automatic mode. If we start, our friend will start moving. And when we press stop, the phone will stop. The user can input the target velocity for the fan over here in this textbooks. Please be aware that the access that we have here, that is the one that we need to control is a modular access and the unit of measurement is the debris. And what specific is that? The user will input our PM velocity. So you will need to manage the fact that the target is in our RPM and the fan axis is working with the degrees per second. And you need to recall that one r.p.m. is equal to six degrees per second. So you will also find a mean program that for you will be empty. This is already the completed exercise. You have an enumeration that I will talk about later. And let's see, the global variable is. And so couple them with the of my. So let's talk about buttons. We have this enable button that is a push button. This means that will be toggled every time you press it. And this is necessary to for the machine to work. So the idea is that if you press enable, you will power on your fan with the M.C power function block. And if you removed enable, it will go off. Then if you are enabled, you can either choose between manual mode or automatic mode. You can do that by pressing these buttons and you have two buttons to jump forward and backward that only work if you are in a manual mode and you have the starting stop button. There are these variables that work only when you are in automatic mode. You have this long real variable that can be used to track the velocity. And as a parameter, we have here that we have a minimum on maximum velocity.

So in your code, you will need to take care of this velocity to be within this range. Then we have some fixed parameters for exploration and a for emergency consideration that we will see how it should work in a moment. Then on the left side, we have an enabled lab that will need to turn on, yeah, whenever the machine is enabled, whenever the fan is enabled. We have a running. Bowling, that is this one that will need to be turned on only if the machine is running it in automatic mode, so it means that the machine is in automatic mode and it has been started. Then we have to that it's too early these that will tell us if the machine is in manual or out mode and these two are controlled by the means of this initiative. This is no motive is simply this one so can be equal to manual or auto. And if you set it one way or another, this that or this one will turn on. Then here we have also an emergency button that is working in negative logic. So to means that the button isn't pressed, that false move means that it is pressed. You will find this that this this is quite typical on machines. And also, you have an alibi for the alarm that will be turned on when an alarm occurs or when the emergency is pressed. If you press the emergency, you will need to also reset by the means of this reset button. So I will go online with a finished project so you can see how it should work. So let me just reset Worm for now. You can see that we are in manual mode right now because we are in one of those too. We cannot be in idle mode. And you can see that whenever I press one of these buttons. The mood switches. If I enabled the machine, we get to this enabled. We've also these two variables, the financial position and the factor velocity that are actually this actual position and actual variables that need to be filled by you by using the read the actual position and read actual velocity. And you also need to take care of the conversion to r.p.m.. So we are in manual mode. What happens if I press the button, the phone will start spinning. For us, the minus. It will spin in the other direction. Our speed is limited between 10 and 100, so if I write zero here, you can see that it gets back to 10. So, right, write value, let's say, 40, it's And you can see that the family's been at 40 r.p.m.. If I write 200, you will see that it will be capped at 100. And this is the maximum speed for a fan. OK, so this is manual mode. And while in outmost, if you press start, you can see that the phone will start there were running late will become true.

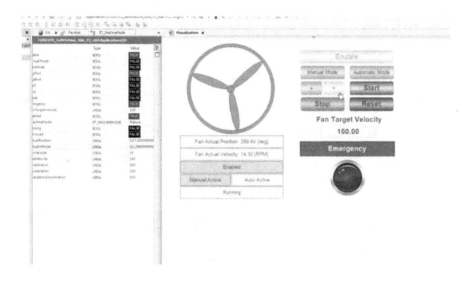

And it will do so until the press stop. If you switch to another mode while you're running, you will be automatically stopped. If you press the emergency button. The fan will first stop. Then it will be disabled and you will not be able to do anything unless you remove the emergency and reset with the reset button. Then you can start again if you press emergency and they remove it and try to start again. You can see that it won't work. And instead, if I reset here. With the emergency press, you can see that the alarm goes off. But I won't be able to enable the machine, so we need to remove it. Then I can start again. And I think the defending needs to be he will have to change the velocity on the fly. So if I write 40 here, you will need we'll see here the speed, the ramping up. And if I turn back again, it will get down. So these are the specifics for the problem for the project. I suggested to try to do it on your own. I suggest a structured text, the state machine approach. But don't worry, in the next few videos, I will carry out this project with you, and I will show you how I did it. Please. There is no on. There is not only one way to do this and are many, so this will be just my take on this.

PROJECT 1 - FAN MOTION - PART 1 - MOTION CONTROL FUNCTION BLOCKS

Let's get to our empty main program, and let's start thinking about how we need to do this. So. We will surely need that to create a state machine for our sequence of operations. So in our main program, I will create the state Bible that I will simply called I call UI state and will be an unsigned integer. Then we will need all the functional blocks for the control of the axis. So let's write down here. AMC function blocks and let's think about what we need, starting with the administrative and diagnostic function blocks. We will surely need a power function lo So how do we create in that be power fan? That will be an AMC power? We will need the diagnostics functional blocks such as reactor opposition, redacted velocity and the axis arrow. But first of all, we will need as an administrative one a reset. So be a reset fan and the type would be AMC reset that we will need the once I told you so you will have 12 position fan B and C lead actor to position, then be a reactor velocity fan and there will be AMC with actual velocity. OK, I guess we want need for now an AMC free status. So we can avoid using it. Then we will meet a few movement functional blocks. So for the manual mode, we will surely need an F and C jog. So B jokes and will be an M.C. jog. For the automatic mode, we will need the maximum velocity, so be velocity fan, and the type would be seen in the city. Then we we also need a functional look to stop yet so this stop fan and a type the AMC stock. I guess that for us, for now, this function looks are quite enough, so in order to divide the two and not make a mess of our program, we create an action within our main program. So and object to action and we create a structure. It takes that action in this way right now because we don't need to mess around with the function blocks. We need to write code to make them work so we won't be forcing any input. So it's OK to use for projects that matter. My opinion and I will call this motion control cause. Below here, so. In our program, that's the way to come and see motion control calls action. Let's cross to the church of this right. Motion control calls semicolon.

OK, so the first thing that our program will do will be to call this all the function looks all the see open motion control function works. So over here in our in our action, we will need to write to the code for this function works. So this will be quite tedious and repetitive, but we need to do that. So. We will is the F2 button, the search for the function books. So first, we need to call the embassy power, so be power firm. And we will be right here. The fennecs is considered this is much faster than the day where you need it to violate all the question marks and so on. And I will leave all the inputs and outputs like this, mostly because I prefer it that way. Some people like to create variables for each input and variables for each output, but I think that this, in my opinion, this is not very useful because you can access this variable using the dot notation anyway, and you will simply create moments in your program. But this is all, in my opinion. Feel free to do however you prefer. So we have the power function lock, then let's see them all over here. We have the reset, so the. Reset. Sen. Let's do this for all of them, and then we will place the axis of the Reed actor position. You have to again. Has he read at The Lost City? Your actual. Here. Then we have the jog function walk. The jog. The velocity that would be move velocity. And that's the stop.

So last place, the fennecs is set in out, viable on all of them. And then we are almost going to go. OK, then let's do another thing, and this is something that you may or may not do for this project, they choose to do this. I will force the enable our hardcoded the enable of this function looks through. So for the reluctant position and velocity because we may as well keep them always through. So we created these values from the axis because we need to. And since we have some fixed the variables for the acceleration and deceleration of the movements, that's also our code that these parameters to the function box. So in the JAG, I will write the R V underscore R acceleration and deceleration. We want to use the jerk, and the same will go for the movie velocity, and we won't do this for the star because we need to choose the or the deceleration or the emergency deceleration, according to the situation that leads to it to the stop. So. This is fine for us, so we are actually calling all the function blocks over here, and we are, let's say, good to go. Oh sorry, I forgot an important function that is Read X's error. So I will add it right here below the after the loss against the FBI asks her to be an emcee in this area. And let's not call for that. Just below the radar blast. So that's the read our practices at power and the axis over a year, well, of course, being able to throw as well. OK, that's good. Then. Let's start down here to brag to our state machine. That's right, something where I'll do so Main Street. A shame. So we can see. From went through the code and over here, we will write case. UI state. Oh, and then over here, we will have our Steve Moshin. So let's start from our state zero, that will be a disabled state. So right here, machine visible state. So. If we are in the Zeeble state, surely we will have this enabled, viable and able levy that is this one. This will surely be off so we can write this in the state. So here I will write enabled. Is equal to falls, and surely we will also have the running tally be equal, this falls. So whenever we are here, we surely are not enabled and we are not threatening.

Then let's think about what we need to do to transition to another state. So in order to get to enable state, we will need to receive the U.S. naval command. So the. GSX Enable will need to be true, but also we will we will not enable the access if we have an emergency, so condition of for a transition from the state will be if we have enable and access emergency. But remember that emergency is a negative logic. So having this variable equal to true means then that the button is not pressed. So if we have in this condition, what do we need to do, we will need to power on our axis. So. We were right here that it. Will be power fed that enabled will need to be set to true. But this is actually the enabled for the function lo So you function block will always need to be running. So we cannot code this here through. And remember that this is only happening for this implementation. Sometimes you are moving the needle as the main function like input. So in other implementations, enable is actually the combination of these two. So over here, we will need to turn on the axis so we need to arrive to the beat drive, start to through and the be a guarantee to. Then we will need to move to another state. So let's say you are a state is equal to five. And here is the five. We should wait for the power to be on. So wait for our arm. Here we will write today if our power fan the status is true, then we are power done. And therefore, then we can move to other states. So let's say that we get to stay 10. And why would they do that? We get the enfeebled feedback equal to truth. And here we have state tests in which we will do something. OK, so we have the transition that enables our machine, and let's also handle the transition that these moves our machine. So this is a transition that women to happen wherever we are in our state machine. So rather than placing a transition in each state, let's add the one outside of the state machine. So over here will like visible transition. And we will write about that if we are not GSX enabled, then. We will force the state to get back to zero, and we will also disable our power, so here have to be power for the. Livestock would be equal to falls and beef our farm, and the beef regulator would be equal to plus. And once we get back here, the neighborhood will be set to be force as well. OK, so let's get online and see how this works. OK, so let's start our Kelsey. Let's get to the visualization. And let's see what happens. So. We are in state zero. We have the emergency rule, and that means that the bottom is impressed. So for Press, enable, OK, we get this al-Liby turned on. I was done and we have the status of the FBI power the truth. And if we get to the finances here, you'll see that we are in the standstill state, so we're ready to move. And if I. Press, you need remove the enable, you can see that we get disabled if we have the emergency press and a press enable you to see that it doesn't work. Later on, we will also manage the transition when we are enabled, and we pressed the emergency that will come later. So we manage the the enabling and disabling of the access.

PROJECT 1 - FAN MOTION - PART 2 - MANUAL MODE

We and how to power on and off the axis right now, we will start managing the manual of the project. But first of all, we will need to actually manage the pressing of these two buttons in order to switch from a mode to another. So while we can do over here before the steam machine, we can write a few lines of code saying that these are lines of code to manual the manual how to buttons, and let's see or hear from the right made global variables. We have a manual mode and auto mode buttons. So if the manual mode? It's true, meaning that the button is being pressed that we will need to set this machine mode to manual. So let's write this in a single line in order to make it more compact. You know it machine mode equal to 80 machine mode that manual semicolon. And if, yeah, we need to do the same for the auto mode. So if the auto mode then hit, the machine mode should be equal to it. Machine mode that auto semicolon and if? So in this way, we will be sure that whenever a button is pressed, this variable will switch volume between manual and auto.

OK, then over here we will need to transition to a certain state if we are in manual mode and to an out of it if we are in auto mode. So I will say that 10 is the manual active state and I would say that 20 is the. Out of active state. So over here, I can write it, if G Machine mode is equal to time machine mode, not manual, then we will need to get two state equal to 10 aisles. That's right. I'll see if it's the same. Let's write it down. In order to make it more clear, if the machine mode instead is auto, then the state will be 20. And if? So we are enabled. And if we get to stay 10, we will need to manage the the manual function of the machine, so. We will need to actually use our FBI job. So let's first take a look at the functional work. For it to work, we will need to link the drug forward and backward that will allow any inputs. And we will also need to specify a velocity for it. So. We have all we hear from our visualization, this LR fund target velocity that is actually in our RPM velocity. So whenever we use the box open AMC codes we have, we use the motion control axis, you know, the velocity is measured using the units per second that in our case, our degrees per second. So we will need to handle this conversion and we will need to say that our velocity for the for the jargon so and be fair, not velocity will need to be our JLR fan target velocity times.

One, our is equal to six degrees per second, and we need to specify the velocity using the degrees per second. Then over here, we also need to start using the the jump forward and backward inputs. So over here we will say that be junk fan. The jog forward would be equal to a global variable jump forward individual fan. No backward would be equal to the G X Junk, Kurt. So in this way, we should be able to move correctly. So let's try it. Let's get on line download. And let's get to our visualization. That's press the Enable button soon as the visualization starts up first is visible once again, sorry, let's try to switch manual and audio. You can see that it works. So let's try to be in auto, and right now we have zero here. We shouldn't be able to have a zero. As I showed you intro in the introduction, but we will see later on how to deal with this. That's right, Tony. And OK, we can see that the fan is moving. And if it really is, I'm moving backwards. OK, it seems to work right now. We are not showing the velocity over here, neither the velocity nor the position, and we will need to take care of this. And also, you can see that we are not limiting the velocity between 10 and hundreds of these two values over here, so we will need to take care of that as well.

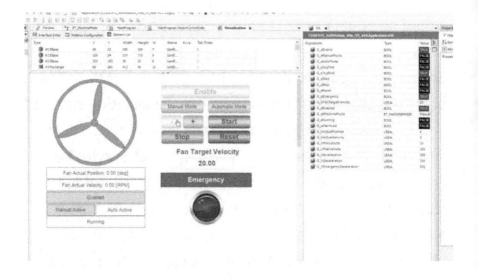

And also right now, if we get to on auto mode, we are still in manual mode, so we will need to manage the transition in the state machine whenever we change the active mode. So let's do that first, let's handle the fact that we are not seeing any position or velocity in our visualization. So we can use our read actual position and read actual velocity. So as you can see in this function blogs, we have this varied output that if we get into the library, so it's in three basic values, we have the diagnostics once and for the reader to a velocity position. Sorry, we have the it's saying that if it is true that it outputs are available. So in our code down here, no, we can't see right here. So codes for updating the actual position and sorry position and, well, velocity, saying that the FDA read the actual position, saying that valid is true, then our JLR actual position will be the first to be re-elected will position the position. The same way we will do the same thing for the grid, the actual velocity fan, the ultraviolet, if the are serve our our actual velocity, the site will be equal to the FBI. Read actual velocity fan dot velocity. But wait, we need to do something more because our function block will return the velocity in the units per second that are degrees per second. And we need that to display the velocity in RPM. So since the one rpm is six degrees per second over here, we will need to divide by six. OK, so that's one thing that we needed to do. We also needed to actively limit the velocity, the target velocity. This one between the minimum and the maximum. And in order to do that, there is a very useful function that is called limit. The limit function will take three inputs a minimum value and maximum value and a current value. And it will return the current value limited between the minimum and the maximum. This can also be written with a simple if statement saying that if the value is below the minimum, it should be equal to the minimum and that if the value is bigger than the maximum, it should be equal to the maximum. But this is a quite compact way to do that. So over here I will write handle target velocity limitation, and I will say here that our goal, our fun target velocity, will be equal to limiting the exactly to our final target velocity between the minimum that is key in velocity and the maximum that is G. Hello, max velocity. Let's go online and see if it works. Carry out a download. Start appeal, see get back to the visualization. We can already see that the velocity is already 10, so it is no longer serious because it's being limited between 10 and 100. And right now, we can try to write zero again, gets equal to 10, then 20, it gets equal 100. OK, that's say, 20. And we are in manual mode. Let's enable and let's move. OK? So you can see it go quite fine. Let's also take a look to our let's open the main program here. Sorry, this one be very pretty. But I want to see the actual value coming out of the FBI. Read the velocity. Is this one? And if we are going to get 20 r.p.m., you can see that we are reading 120 over there on the top right. Because it means actually 120 degrees per second. That means that one turn every three seconds is actually 20 per minute. OK, that's nice. And moving back, it works in the same way. And unless changes the velocity to 10, you can see that it will move at 10. Let's also add another another little modification. So that is needed, actually, because right now we are working on the screen and we can click one thing at a time. But we also need to take into account the fact that we may click on more than one thing at the same time. So for instance, if I disabled, if I am able to disable the axis while we are jogging, you can see that we will not be able to reset this dock forward and jump backward because we will directly transition to state zero. So in this transition, I need also to make sure that our Jack fan not jump forward will be equal to force and be a fan, not jump backward will be equal to false as well that we need to manage the transition between the outer auto state and the job state. So. Whenever we transition between manual inactive, we'll need to make sure that the fan has stopped so. Let's say that we use let's see over here, steep 60, a big enough number that will be our transition minor to active or sorry manner to our top or auto to manual. And over here, we will say that if we are manual state and. We change machine mode. So machine mode gets equal to a time machine mode, not auto. Then we will need to stock the fan and get to the state. So I will say that first, we need to set the junk forward and backward, the inputs to force in order to abort any drug operation that may be going on. And then we will need to call the FBI stop. Fan. So I would see a fully stocked fan not executed equal to true, and I would need to set the celebration as well because we didn't do that in the election and we didn't do that in the election because we may need to switch between the deceleration one or the sorry, the standard one or the emergency one. And in this case, we need the standard one. So f b stuck fan thought the situation would be equal to g o r discoloration. OK, then we will need to transition to our state. Sixty. In state 60, we will wait for the for the access to stop and then we will transition to the other state. So why we need to do is simply to check if this stop has finished. So I read that right that if stop the the f a b stop fan not done, then first of all, we will need to set the execute force. And since we are using a single state to transition to Arto or to manual, I will check again here that if we are setting the machine mode to be equal to our time. So if machine mode auto, then we will need to transition to state to any. Guess that's what I tell Steve, yet machine mode equal to 80 machine mode manual, then the seat will be equal to 10. Again, we don't need this. I'll see if I'm also I'm doing this in the case that we don't know. Maybe one day you will have another mode, and if you add a little model, we would all in. One need to modify this code because you are actually looking at the fact that the machine mode is equal to a specific value. So in this transition state, we will stop and we will get to 20 if we transition to auto and to 10 if we transition to two manual and we will need to do something similar to this. Also in this 20 state, so yes, I will write here in the state 10 that this is the transition to auto mode. So transition to auto mode and here instead 20, I will need to have something similar. So I will copy this and paste it here. We will need to transition to manual mode and we will need to do this if the mode has become equal to manual. We won't need to reset the JAG, but over here we will use the move velocity. We don't need to reset the execute of the move velocity if needed. OK, so let's see if we are able to transition between these two modes again. Let's carry out download. Visualization. OK, you close it. Reopen it again. I enabled the access. We are my role model. We will find that transition to automatic mode. You can see that my job comments no longer work because we are state 20 where state 20, but we got there by getting to state 60 in which we stopped the access. Right now, if I get to manual mode, we get to speak 10, and we did this in the same way because we got it to the FBI. We gave an execute coming to the FBI stop. And since the access war was already in standstill, the done was immediate. So in this lesson, we manage the few things we manage, the transitions we manage, the velocity of mutation and the velocity and position display.

PROJECT 1 - FAN MOTION - PART 3 - AUTO MODE

So let's start to look now at the auto mode. So we got here instead, Tony. And in automotive, we will start using the move velocity function black. And in order to be consistent, let's also add another condition over here that if we are getting back to the two stage zero where we disable everything, we should also set the move velocity, execute the falls, he noted, to be consistent and be sure that whenever we start or the function blocks executes are on faults. OK, so let's manage the auto procedure. Since we are using an execute function blocks, we will need to spread this on many states and we the specific is that when we are in auto mode, we need to wait for a start, for a start button and being pressed. So what we will need to do this will be state training in which we are not a mode and we are waiting for the start. We may have the transition to the manual mode, but over here we will see that if we have the start button being pressed. We should move this state, let's say, state twenty five. And as we do that, since we are starting the machine, we will need to set the running. This one, the true. OK, then what we need to do is take 25 will be to actually start the mobile city functional lo So here we will write out of. So you start with the velocity and over here as well, we will say that we will need to feel the inputs of the move velocity function lo So we'll need to see that the FBI move velocity fan that velocity will need to be equal to the global variable that is JLR. Fan target, the velocity that needs to be converted to the Greens per second, so time six.

```
      1  PROGRAM MainProgram
      2  VAR
      3      uiState       :    UINT;
      4
      5      // MC Function Blocks
      6      fbPowerFan              :        MC_Power;
      7      fbResetFan              :        MC_Reset;
      8      fbReadActualPositionfan :        MC_ReadActualPosition;
      9      fnReadActualVelocityfan :        MC_ReadActualVelocity;
     10      fbReadAxisError         :        MC_ReadAxisError;
     11      fbJogfan                :        MC_Jog;
     12      fbMoveVelocityFan       :        MC_MoveVelocity;

     46              fbStopFan.Deceleration := G_lrDeceleration;
     47              uiState := 40;
     48          END_IF

     54      //**** Auto Active - Wait for Start
     55      20:
     56          IF G_xStart THEN
     57              uiState := 21;
     58              G_xRunning := TRUE;
     59          END_IF

     61          // Transition to Manual Mode
     62          IF G_etMachineMode = ET_MachineMode.Manual THEN
     63              fbMoveVelocityFan.Execute := FALSE;
     64              fbStopFan.Execute := TRUE;
     65              fbStopFan.Deceleration := G_lrDeceleration;
     66              uiState := 40;
     67          END_IF

     69      //**** Auto Active - Start MoveVelocity
     70      25:
     71          fbMoveVelocityFan.Velocity := G_lrfanTargetVelocity|

     75      //*** Transition Manual --> Auto or Auto --> Manual
     76      40:
     77          IF fbStopFan.Done THEN
     78              fbStopFan.Execute := FALSE;
```

And we will also need to set that direction and we can accord it as well. So here I will write that the direction is AMC direction the positive because we will always move in positive direction. And therefore, here I need to say that velocity there needs to be said through. OK, then what do we need to do? We need to get to a state. Thirdly, let's say and in the state, we will need to wait for the for the velocity imputed to become through to know whether or not we have reached the target velocity. So over here we will say, oh, two active state 30 will be all too active. Um, wait for in velocity. And we were moved to stay 30 as soon as it would be a functional block. The embassy move velocity will start working. So as soon as we have the the busy output, so here I will say right that if the f b move velocity fan that busy is true, then state will become equal to 30. And this will be a transition given by the fact that to move velocity is working and I think we will need to allow over here as well. The transition to the manual mode so we can copy and paste this transition over here. And one thing we need to take care of is that we will need to set the big banks running equal to false. If we transition to manual otherwise, the lady this lady here will remain turned on. So we need to have this transition in all the states concerned with art mode. OK, so get to state 30 and in state 30 since we are our function clock is already running. We can reset the move velocity execute. We will reset the velocity execute, and we will wait for the sole wait for the velocity reached. So if we have the velocity fan not in velocity, then our state should be, let's say, 40. And for us, state 40 will be the one in which. We'll be out of active velocity or. And in both of these states, we need to copy the transition to the manual mode. So.

Right now, let's go online and try this out. The stars sort of deal, see, and let's try the automatic mode start, OK? We can see that the fan is moving and it is fine. Right now, we have no way to stop it with the stop button. The other way we have to stop for now is to switch to man on the moon and back to order. Let's change the velocity and let's say 2:20 start and this starts and we should be in state. 40. Yeah. And we can also see that if we update to the velocity here, there was no effect. So we should manage that.

And in order to do so, let's go back off line. And what do we need to do here in our function? Look in our mean velocity as we know it will change the velocity with the rising ends of the executed. So what we need to do, we need to keep, track and check if the velocity that we set here has changed. So whenever the function is running, whenever the more velocity is running, we will need to look to check if the the velocity value has changed. So we stay 30 and instead 40. We will need to see if the velocity has changed. So here is 30. I will write a velocity change transition that won't be even by the fact that if the FBI move velocity fan that velocity and that is the one we stored here when we started the function block is different from the value that we set it to. And this only may only occur if this value changes and this can change that can be changed from the HMRC. So if these two values are different, we will need to give another rising edge to the execute. So we need to get back to state 25 in which we set to be executed through in this needs to occur as well when we are in state. 40. Let's see how it works. Again, that's carry out download. OK, visualization. Let's first enable the machine as soon as the position starts. Auto mode start and let's change the value and right to training. As you can see, after a small ramp, the velocity gets to 20. That's right, 100. And as you can see, the fans start spinning faster and faster. That's right. 50. You can see it ramps down as well. So we are almost there. We need to stop. We need to be able to stop. And we can do that at the moment, only switching to manual mode. But we need to be able to do that with the stop button as well. So in our machine, we will need to also add the transition to stopping state. So let's say that we are 50 state, 50 will be our. Stopping state for the out auto mode, so auto activity stuffing state. And therefore, in all of these states, so state 25, 30 and 40, we will need to allow this transition. So I will right over here. Stop requests. So if we get a stop request, it means that we have the next stop vulnerable people the truth, then we will need to first to reset the running global. We need to reset those on the move velocity fan execute to falls. We will need to set the FBI Stop X stuff and to execute equal to true as well as the deceleration. And since this is a standard stopping procedure, we will need to set it to the jihadist operation and not to the emergency one. We need to do that and then we need to move to state 50. That will be the state in which we will wait to stop. And this transition needs to occur also in state 30 and the state 40. So that copy and paste it here. And here. OK, that is state 50, we need to write something that is pretty similar to what we have in six states 60. So in the state, 15, we will have that if we have the FBI stop. Fan done -- heavy stuff, and the executed can be reset to false. And the state can go back to the state in which we wait for the start, that is state 20. So this is fine for us. Let's try and see if it works. OK, let's start the see that visualization. Let's enable automatic mode start, let's press stop so we can see stops. Let's see, here we are on stage 20, so this is fine and we can do whatever we want now we can get to speed 40. We can stop, but we can get manual mode. Forward, just backwards. And then back to auto mode start. Getting back to manual mode can move to do it fast in here if I switch from oh to and start, yeah. Nonstop. So this works fine, we need to just to had a simple thing, we need to get here. Yes, we in the part in which we disable everything and in order to be consistent, in order to avoid that logs, we need to also cried if we stop execute two falls. Because if somehow we disable the machine when the execute is through and we don't resent it, then we won't be able to start because the executives are blocking is a locking function block. So this is fine for us. We are almost done when you manage both the manual and auto mode. The next lesson we will just see how to manage the emergency..

PROJECT 1 - FAN MOTION - PART 4 - EMERGENCY MANAGEMENT

We need to manage the emergency or alarm stop for defense so this this transition should occur no matter what is the state in which we are. So we will manage the transition outside the state machine. So we will say out here that if we have the emergency quota, the false meaning that the emergency button, these press or we have an or so it's a function block reflexes are not error. If we have one of these two and we are not visible. Then we need to cause an emergency stop. So over here, we will write FBI stuff and not execute will be set to true. And this time we will need to use the emergency this operation so the situation input will be equal to JLR, an emergency declaration. Since this is a transition that may occur in any other state, we need to make sure to respect both the jog and move velocity and executes. So I will copy these three lines from the simple translation. We need to maintain the motor enabled, so we won't use this too. And we need to get to another state. So let's say state gets equal to 100 and this will be in the emergency English our transition. Here we will have our state 100. There will be the. Emergency. Which we will need to stop. So we have already set the execute of the emergency through here, and we did this here in order to be faster. So so in a way that we avoid waiting for a cycle before sending the execute to through to the function block. So since we are in an emergency state, we also need to set the VAT bill, I am putting that is this one that is actually the.

Alarm at the marble, so here as we do all this, I will also set this to true. And we need to stop the function, the axis, so here we will wait for the FBI, stop Van de Don to be equal to Trump. And as soon as we have done that, have fans that execute this stuff and then execute will be set to false and we will move to another state that's a hundred and ten and relent in the state 110 once we have successfully stopped. Yes, this we will need to disable them. So here I would write emergency disabling and I will write an FBI power fan not being restored equal to force have b power fan that meet the regulator on equal to force in order to be sure that our access is disabled. I will wait for the FBI power fame that status to be equal to false. Then let's move to another state, St. Andre, in training. So whenever the emergency button is pressed, we will. Then after that, to resume the operation, we will need to receive a reset request from the army. So he state 20 sorry, state 120 will be our emergency wait for reset state. And over here, we will say that if we get the reset equal to true. We will need to chew things if we have an error. We will need to resign, otherwise we can go back to state zero. So. I will say that if we have an hour or so, if FBI relaxes Sarah that area, then we will need to use the MSI reset to reset the the access error. So we'll see a big reset that you reset from not executed is equal to true. And I will need to get into another state. Oh, it's we wait for the deed done output of the reset function so U.S. state is equal in 30. And in St. one hundred and thirty, I would say this is an emergency wait for reset done. And here if we reset fan got done, then we can get back to state zero. Otherwise, if we do not have any error to reset, we can get back directly to state zero and as soon as we get back into state zero, we can write it here. The alarm led me to get set to false. Over here and over here. Just another thing, if we were right to this transition this way.

```
FileMenu    ET MachineMode    IA    MainProgram.MotionControlCalls    MainProgram X    Library Manager    Visualization    GVL
    PROGRAM MainProgram
    VAR
        uiState    :    INT;

        // #C_Function Blocks
        fbPowerFan            :    #C_Power;
        fbResetFan            :    #C_Reset;
        fbReadActualPositionFan   :    #C_ReadActualPosition;
        fbReadActualVelocityFan   :    #C_ReadActualVelocity;
        fbReadAxisError       :    #C_ReadAxisError;
        fbJogFan              :    #C_Jog;
        fbMoveVelocityFan     :    #C_MoveVelocity;
    END_IF

    //*** Emergency - Wait for Reset
    100:
        IF Q_xReset THEN
            IF fbReadAxisError.Error THEN
                fbResetFan.Execute := TRUE;
                uiState := 110;
            ELSE
                G_xDisabled := FALSE;
                uiState := 0;
            END_IF
        END_IF

    //*** Emergency - Wait for Reset Done
    110:
        IF fbResetFan.Done THEN
            Q_xDisabled := FALSE;
            uiState := 0;
        END_IF
    END_CASE

    // Disable Prevention
    IF NOT G_xEnable THEN
        fbPowerFan.bRegulatorOn := FALSE;
        fbPowerFan.bEnable := FALSE;
        fbMoveVelocityFan.Execute := FALSE;
        fbJogFan.JogForward := FALSE;
        fbJogFan.JogBackward := FALSE;
```

We can see that whatever the state in whatever state we are, we will get state one on one. This means that if we get to state one and entitlement, we will force this transition to statewide and back again. So we need to disable this transition if we are already processing an emergency. So simple way to do that. We will write that if the state that we need this state to be also lower than the 100 in this way, since we used this 100, 110, 120 130. We can't force this way. It would be actually more precise to write state. It is not equal to one hundred and ten and so on. But actually, this works as well. So let's try it out. Let's go back online to download. And let's start the policy, and then we will try our emergency bottom. So we will try in and we'll try it out in different conditions, in different situations, so. Let's see. If we pressed the emergency bottom when we are disabled, nothing will occur. But and

120

we will just be not be able to get back. So this is fine for us if we have the machine enabled. We can see that we get to this whole red light. And if I remove the emergency and press reset, we are good to go. So let's move, let's get to automatic mode and start. Let's press the emergency button. Something isn't quite right because we shouldn't be disabled. So let's see who we are in state. 120. So, OK, so we forgot to remove the flag. The G.S. enabled flag. So this is what we should do. So let's get back on flying. And when we get the status quo to Force X in the booth, it's to be equal to force as well. OK, so let's get back online. Visualization. Right now, we should yeah, OK, so we are not in that state. So let's try it again. We said. Some of the emergency and start. Emergency, OK, we get enable equal the force. They remove the emergency button and reset. Now I'm able to start again. Manual mode emergency will get disabled since we are already still reset and we cannot move because we do not, we have the emergency still pressed. Auto mode start. OK, so this is fine for us. It seems to work quite well. And we actually did everything according to the facts. So we are able to manage this machine in auto mode. We can update the velocity on the fly. We are using the continuous motion function blocks in the correct way. We are using the stop ones as well in the correct way, and we can see the difference in the ramp. The emergency ramp is much faster and we also mean that's all the flow for this simple machine. So we work the logic and the logic code to manage all this operate in all this machine modes and ways of functioning. And as you saw, even if it is a simple thing and there are quite a lot of things that needs that we need to take care of. So this is the end of this project, and we will get back to our basic project to our playground. Let's see, and we will start to take a look at discrete motion functional blocks.

INTRODUCTION TO DISCRETE MOTION

We will get back to our motion controls basic project, and we will start to talk about discrete motion in the previous section. We have taken a look at continuous motion, and continuous motion is one type of motion that has no clear end and can go on indefinitely. Discrete motion instead is a type of motion that as a clear start and the clear and and descriptive motion function blocks are typically used for position, profile, movement. So moving from one position to another and taking a look at the PRC open state diagram, you can see that for discrete motion you, we will get into the discrete motion PRC open state.

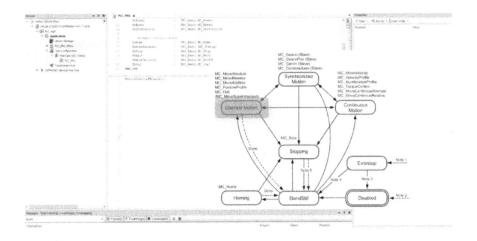

If you get use and execute of these motion function block and then you can get back to the standstill state as soon as you have done output of the function block. Of course. And this motion function block can be interrupted by the AMC stop. And this is the reason you can see a clear line from this great emotional state to the stopping state. But the typical way to use this crude motion function block is to start it. Would you execute and wait for it done output? That means that the positioning movement is finished.

ABSOLUTE POSITION PROFILE (MC_MOVEABSOLUTE)

We will start to take a look at one of the most used function blocks of four discrete motion in the PRC open standard, and that is the move absolute function block first so we can take a look at it in the library manager. So if you select as a as in the previous video, the SM three basic library, you get the same three basic plus movement. And over here you will have the IMSI absolute function block with all the documentation regarding it, and this functional look is used to move an axis to an absolute position. OK, so. Let's start to add it to our project, and let's also try it, so let's get to our main program. And just below this definition, let's add the move velocity. So here I will say have beaten move, so remove absolutely remove. Absolute with will be an awesome three. Basic Dart M.S. Move Absolute. So let's get back to our motion control function, because. And let's get below the latest functional block that we added. That was the AMC jog. And over here. I will write here, F.B. move. Absolutely. As always, rest remove the question marks. And let's add the axis over here. So in this project right now, we have a finite axis. And let's see how this works. And let's take a look at the inputs and outputs, so the outputs are quite standard. We have the execute input that will start the movement and therefore will lead to a transition from a standstill state or from another state to the discrete motion state. We have a position, a target position that is our target for the movement. So this function look will carry out what is called the trapezoidal, trapezoidal positioning profile. This means that it will have an acceleration phase, a constant velocity phase and then a deceleration phase until it gets to the target position that we specify. We may also use a jerk. So jerk is the derivative of acceleration and can be used to have a smoother profile for the acceleration. But actually, we want to do that in this course, and we have this direction input that we will talk about later on. And this is only used for modulo axis. And then we have the buffer mode that also is not part of the standard. There are not a lot of implementation that use it. So I will not talk about that. OK, so we have placed our function black all over here. Let's go online. So I started my policy. I will enable the drive. Let's also enable our.

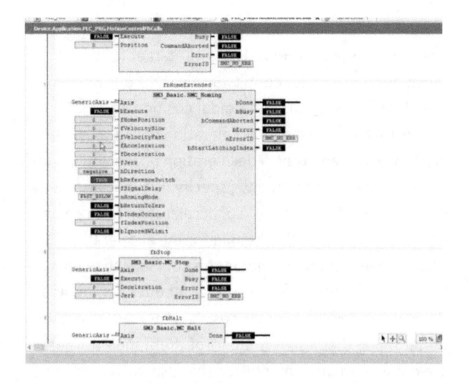

Diagnostic function books, so read status, reactor velocity or reactor position, but the main one for us right now is red status. And let's also start our trace. OK, so I have the trace running here on my right side, and we need also to take a look at what happens when we start the movement. So over here we have the position that the velocity and the acceleration. So the red one is the position, green one is velocity and blue is acceleration. So right now we are at position zero and we are still. And let's say that we want to get the position. Let's see 100. So what? I would write 100 in the position input of the AMC move. Absolute function. Look, let's choose a velocity. So something small enough. So let's say 20. In this way, we should take around five seconds to get there. Let's choose an acceleration of 20 and an X deceleration of 10. In this way, it would take one second to get maximum velocity and to second to decrease to velocity zero. And we will see what happens right now. And since we have a finite axis, we won't care about that direction. And let's see what happens. So if I raise the execute well first, I would be over here so you can see that it will get into the discrete motion phase. So right now, where we'd be pressing control and seven. And as you can see. Let's wait for it to end, and then we are back into standstill, so. I will stop the trace so we can take a look at it. And here you can see that you we have our done our part and this done output will remain true until we remove the execute. So let's see what happened. We started from position zero and we got the position hundred. That's exactly what we wanted. We have an acceleration of 20. This is the first phase of the trapezoid and this is the part in which we are accelerating. So we want to reach Velocity 20, and we are doing it by using an acceleration of 20 units per second squared. And if we take a look here, we can place two cursors in the trees. So if you use right click cursor and click cursor again and you are able to place two cursors. And here he will see what is the difference in time. So, um, you may also see what are the values of the variables in the two cursors. But actually, here you can see that it takes one second to reach the maximum velocity with acceleration.

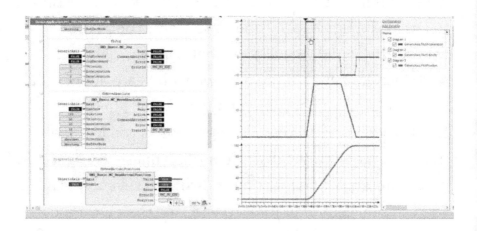

Because we are raising the acceleration of 20 units per second squared. And our velocity is our target velocity is 20 units per second and we carry out the movement at custom velocity then. The decelerating phase starts, and if we measure how long it takes, it would be around two seconds. And you can see here two seconds, 74 milliseconds. This is also due to how I position the cursor. So actually, here we have three phases acceleration, constant velocity deceleration, and at the end we end up in the target position. OK, so let's try something different. Let's have the elevation of 20 here. So we have the same acceleration and deceleration. And let's get to position and within 50. Execute. OK, here the trapezoid is ended, so we are at position 150. Let's try to get back to 100 and we will see the axis moving backward. So velocity is negative, acceleration is negative and deceleration is positive. So this remember this is the position. So we actually did the opposite of what we did before. This is how you move an axis. So let's try to get also to some limit case. So right now, you can see that we have a clear acceleration, constant velocity and the celebration, but let's say that we are in a case in which we do not have enough time to reach the velocity. What will happen then? So let's say that we want to get to the position and understand five from our position of 500. And let's send it racing trigger for the execute. You can see that right now, the. Velocity profile seems more like a triangle because we didn't reach the maximum velocity that we wanted of 20, because the distance we have to move was was actually a lot smaller. So. This is our Twerks Velocita exhibition, and the celebrations should always be positive, and in this way you can get to the absolute value of your position. So you want to move to 100 feet. Sorry, sorry, let's move to a 1000. Feel free to do so. And actually, this movement can be preempted. So if you send another execute for with another position, this will be overwritten. So let's say I want to go to zero and. I will. Send an execute while we are moving toward 100. You can see that the movement has been interrupted and the axis is right now moving to zero. Let's do it again, let's say we want to get to 2000 right now with the same velocity and acceleration and a new positioning profile starts. And you also can send a new execute by if you just want to change the dynamic parameters. So let's say that something happened and we want to move faster. I will change the velocity 60 and I will. Given another execute at the function book and you can see that we are still moving toward 200, sorry, 2000. But the velocity has increased. And let's wait until we get to the to the target position. And we are here. OK, so I will also show you what happens if we send an executed to a position that we already are in. You can see that the axis doesn't move and we get it done output immediately.

ABSOLUTE POSITION PROFILE PER MODULO AXES

We have seen how the muscles function block works right now. We will take a look on seeing out who works for a modular axis. So before going online, we will get over here into our access parameters and we will choose a modular axis with a model, the value of 360. So we're saying that these, let's say, rotate five axis and we are actually looking at the degrees of rotation. So. Let's go online again. With a download. Let's get to our function blocks, so we enable the access. I will enable the read status as well, and I will start the trees over here on the right side. OK, so we are positioned zero velocity, zero acceleration zero. The thing is over here that when we are doing it in absolute motion profile for a modulo axis, there is not only a single way to do so. So for instance, let's say that we have right now, we are at zero degrees, our position is zero degrees. And let's say that we want to move to 90 degrees. We could go forward with a distance of 90 degrees and then stop. But actually, we could do it another way. We could go backward with a for a distance of 270 degrees. So actually, you can get to the same position for what concerns your modulo in two ways. So, for instance, let's right here and let's see the velocity of 16 acceleration 16. And disillusioned 60. So let's select the positive direction. Control and if so. Start. OK, we got to 90 degrees. Let's say that we want to get to 120. We are all 120 over here. Let's write 90 again. What do you think should happen if we had Eleanor access? We will simply go backward to 90 instead of since we have a modular access and we have a directional input set to positive. What will happen is that the access will move forward. It will get to 360, then to zero and back to 90. So we have taken the longest way to get there. So stop the crease. And I will get to the library just to show you what are the possibilities for direction. So again, let's get back to the pro-EU movement. AMC move up. And if we get to that direction, but the type is AMC direction. You can see over here that we have positive negative short tests. That means that it will move in the direction, that means that it will lead to the shortest distance. We have current that he uses the previous one that we used and we also have this fastest and the fastest is actually similar to shortest.

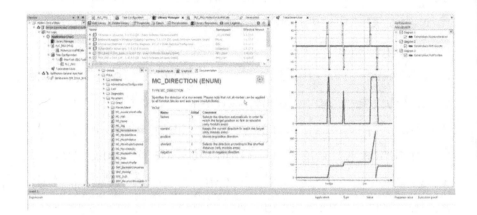

So it means that it will choose the direction that it will lead you to reach the target in the far in the smallest amount of time. And if you start from a standstill position, it will mean that it is the same of using the shortest. But instead, if you are moving, if you are starting a movement and you are already moving fast, this could mean different things could be different from shortest because it you may need to stop as well. So that will take would be computed in the amount of time it needs to get into a position. But let's get back to us and let's try something. OK, so if we are position 90 and if I select shortest, we will always move in the shortest way. So let's say that I want to get to position 300. In order to do so. If we wanted to get to 300 moving forward, it would take me 210 degrees instead if I'm moving backwards. It would take 90 plus 60, that is under then 50. So if I use shortest. It should move backward. Because this is the shortest way to get the position three hundred and again here, if I were 30, if we wanted to get there and moving forward, it would take me 90 degrees by moving backward. It would take me 270. So if I use. Shortest. You can see that access is moving forward. And I can also use negative that is the same way, same thing that we had before. But in the opposite way, so if we wanted to get to position, let's say 40 and we are 30, the axis will do almost a complete turn to get there. We were at 30 and we started moving backward until we reached 40 again. So this is our the direction that input works. It is something that is necessary for modular access because as you may, there is not only one way to get to a position. You can move forward, you can move backward.

RELATIVE POSITION PROFILE (MC_MOVERELATIVE, MC_MOVEADDITIVE)

We will take a look at another very popular function block for this Greek movement. And this is the AMC move relative. So let's first take a look at it in the library manager. We have the EMC move relative over here, and this is used to command a movement of a specified distance. So in this way, we will take we will carry out the movement and the this. We will have a distance that we want to to run and we will not move to an absolute position, but we will move to a relative position. So let's take a look at it. That's created AMC Move Relative. The type is the same three basic AMC move relative. Let's add it over here. Box. F.B. move, relative. The access is this one, and let's remove all the question marks, as always. You can see that the interface is very similar to the move. Absolutely. We have a little differences. First, we do not have the direction input because the issue we had before for the modular axis is something that we do not have when we are talking of relative movements and we do not no longer have the position input, but we have the distance input. So this function block will will make it will start a position profile relative to the position that we have at the moment of the start. So let's go online and test it out. Start. Let's download Trace and less enable the function of the axis. Sorry. This one as well, and as always, was the read status. But you actually have seen only worse when we send an executive. We'll get to this quick motion and then we will get back. OK, so. That's right here in the distance, for instance. That's right. Hundreds, let's say 20, acceleration 20 and deceleration 20. OK, let's start it. OK, we have got to position one. So this seems like the same of the move, absolutely.

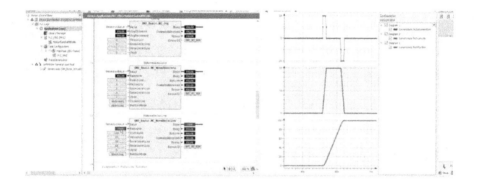

But wait, if we do it again with the same parameters. You can see that it will start moving again. So actually, the target position is the position that we had when we started the movement. Plus the distancing put. So if I wanted to move back to 100, I would need to right here minus 100. And I will start again. And you can see the axis moves back. Let's do it again, minus 100. And execute. Now you can see how it works. OK, so I will show you just another thing. Let's lower the velocity and less of a distance that is 100, so when under the end velocity is 10. So if I start this function block, let's try to see what happens if we give to rising edges of a execute. So. Execute, it starts here. Let's send it again. It keeps on moving, but actually, you can see. That it gets over. And it stopped in this weird position that, in my case, is a hundred and sixty five. And why did this stop here? It stopped here because it seems that I send the execute when it was at 65. So the sampling of the target position happens when you raise the execute. So this can also be used to abort movements and to get to a normal position. So this is one odd behavior. This is not something that is unexpected and this is something you should be aware of if you start a relative movement when you are moving, the target position is computed from the actual position of the axis. So this is the move relative.

RELATIVE POSITION PROFILE (MC_MOVEADDITIVE)

We will take a look at the functional look that is very similar to the move relative, and this functional look is the move additive. So let's add it over here and then I will show you what is the it's actual difference from the move relative. Of additive. Sorry, I had to be messed up over here and. Let's also add the call of the function block. So let's get to our motion control because below the move, relatively without a new network. A new box this will be called FBI Move Additive. Without the access. Over here. Removal, the question marks, as always. And let's go online, and you will see that the interface of the function look is pretty much the same. It doesn't have the buffer mode, but we are not talking about that and it's actually mostly the same function block. So let's add a less the trace and more meat here on the side. And let's try to make a movement, let's say distance 100 situation.

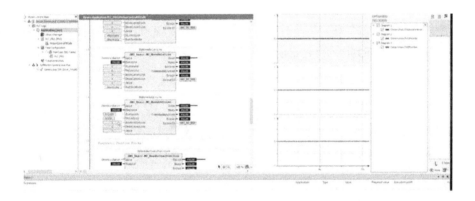

The situation and velocity equals to 20. And let's raise the execute a sorry, I didn't enable the access and this actually is right. Celebrity status as well. I think I need to raise the reset for my case. So. Okay. And let's start it, OK? It's moving. It's getting to 100. And it stops. Let's do it again. Execute the falls, execute the. And as you can see, it seems to be doing the exact same thing that the move relative was doing. So let's get to minus 200, so it means that we'll get to position zero. And as you can see, it seems to be doing the same thing of move relative, actually. It's meant to be the function block is almost the same. And I will show you right now the only difference. Let's make a positioning with a distance of 100 units and a velocity of 10 units. So I will start it, OK? And while I'm doing it, let's give another rising trigger. So if you remember that in the movie, relative, it simply sampled the position when I when I raised the executed and it moved by 100 units and it got around 160. The move additive instead, you can see that it gets to 200 and this is a precise measurement. If I use the cursor, I can show you here, the position is 200. And why is that the move additive will sample the target position based on the current target position? So if you want to carry out of movement with a distance that is 100, it will get to the target position that is the current target position plus 100 plus the distance instead of the move relative sample the current accurate position. So the real position of the axis and that added the distance. So this is the difference between the move relative and move additive. And if you go to the documentation here, people use movement as you move additive. You can see that the target position can result from a proceeding motion of move additive that was aborted, so. If you are bought a position in profile with a move additive, you will use the you will actually care about the first target position and you will add the new distance to the previous one. So this is the main difference. You can see that these two blocks are mostly the same. And with the combination of the move absolute move relative and move additive, you can do almost all your positioning profiles, all the positioning profiles that you want.

PROJECT 2 - CARRIER MOTION - PART 1 – INTRODUCTION

We will take a look at the exercise project for discreet motion. So the layout is very similar to what we had in the continuous motion exercise, so we can see that the interface is pretty much the same. And the main difference is that we do not have a fan axis, but we have a carrier. This carrier is a linear, finite axis and that we can see over here that is range. It goes from minus 50 to 1050. And if we get into the visualization right now, I can try to show you how this works. So this is the complete program. So is the target of the exercise. And later on, I will show you what will be the starting point for you. So. Going online and starting, this is work you should have. And well, we will still have the manual and automatic mode in the same way that we had in the first exercise, and we have the possibility to enable and disable the access as well. For what concerns the manual mode? Well, over here on the left, you can see that you can set up the velocity of the axis and in manual mode you can do a positive or negative jog.

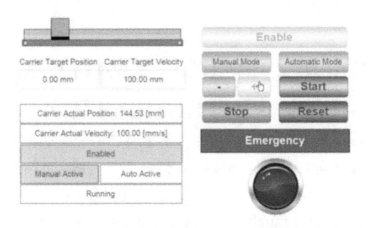

So this part, it works. Mostly in the same way that it did for the for the fan, so we will not need to rewrite this. You will find in the starting project the mental coda that is already written in the main program. Now getting to automatic mode. How does this work? It is meant to carry out two positioning profiles, one that goes at zero and one that goes at target position that can be of choice. So if I write 200 here, I get into automatic mode. The first thing that my program should do, it should move the axis to zero. Then it should start doing a positioning profile to 200 and to zero again, 200 and zero again. And whenever I change the value of the target position, it should take it up at the next cycle. So let me show you what I mean if we start. It will get to zero. And two hundred and zero. 200 and so on. If I write fifty here, when the cycle starts again, you can see that it goes from zero to 50. If I want to raise the velocity, let's say 200. He tries to move faster if I increase the length. It will get to 500 and then come back. The maximum range should be 1000. And this is our work. So if you stop, it will stop whenever it is moving, giving can get back to manual mode and back into automatic mode. Start again. In the same way, if you have a pressing emergency, you will have a steeper ramp to stop. And if you reset the emergency and pressed the reset button, you should be able to start again. So this is very similar to what we had in the first exercise. The only difference is that we will be using the discrete motion function blocks to achieve this movement in the automatic mode. And we will see how to do that, either with the move absolute or with a combination of move absolute and move relative.

PROJECT 2 - CARRIER MOTION - PART 2 - INTRO TO CODE

We will take a look and see how the project is structured and what is the interface and what is the code that is already written for you in the main program? So let's take a look at the interface. Here in the global variable list, you will have in the list of buttons and the list of feedbacks, that is pretty much the same that you had in the fan exercise. So you can enable the access, said the manual or auto mode, the jog forward or backward, the start or stop the automatic cycle pressing emergency or reset an arrow. And you can set the target velocity and the target position for the axis. And the target position is the furthest distance that will be travelled in the automatic cycle and area of the feedbacks that are the same from as the one from the exercise. You have the minimax position that you need to limit the target position that is set from the edge of my. Minimum velocity, again, that you can use to limit the target velocity, acceleration and deceleration and emergency deceleration. And let's take a look at what the code looks like in implementation.

```
VAR_GLOBAL
    // HMI Buttons - Commands
    G_xEnable                     :   BOOL;
    G_xManualMode                 :   BOOL;
    G_xAutoMode                   :   BOOL;
    G_xJogFwd                     :   BOOL;
    G_xJogBwd                     :   BOOL;
    G_xStart                      :   BOOL;
    G_xStop                       :   BOOL;
    G_xReset                      :   BOOL;
    G_xEmergency                  :   BOOL := TRUE;
    G_lrCarrierTargetPosition     :   LREAL;
    G_lrCarrierTargetVelocity     :   LREAL;

    // HMI Leds - Feedback
    G_xEnabled                    :   BOOL;
    G_etMachineMode               :   ET_MachineMode;
    G_xRunning                    :   BOOL;
    G_xAlarmed                    :   BOOL;
    G_lrActualPosition            :   LREAL;
    G_lrActualVelocity            :   LREAL;

    // Global Parameters
    G_lrMinPosition               :   LREAL    := 0.0;
    G_lrMaxPosition               :   LREAL    := 1000.0;
    G_lrMinVelocity               :   LREAL    := 10.0;
    G_lrMaxVelocity               :   LREAL    := 200.0;
    G_lrAcceleration              :   LREAL    := 100.0;
    G_lrDeceleration              :   LREAL    := 200.0;
    G_lrEmergencyDeceleration     :   LREAL    := 500.0;

END_VAR
```

So if you get into the main program. Let's take a lo It is
very similar to the implementation that we developed for
defense exercise, so I didn't want you to redo any of the
work that you already did. So as the variables, you can
see that we have just the state variable and our trigger to
detect the rising edge of the start. We have the power
function of absolute and relative stuff. Jog and diagnostics
function blocks. All the function blocks are called in here.
And it is pretty pretty much the same that we had in the
exercise, removing the part from the for the automatic
mode. So you can see that down here, the disabled
transition, emergency transition, whatever we did in

defense, exercise is already implemented. We have the emergency part. We have the manual mode here and you can see that over here. This is where you should write your own code for the automatic mode. So you would need to you see here that you should get to state 20 when you select automatic mode. And you should handle the transition back in your states. So right now, the only thing that is implemented is the manual mode, so it should work fine. And right now, we should try to implement the automatic mode using the function blocks, remove absolute or a combination of move absolute and move around you. So I suggested to try to do this on your own and see what you are able to do and what are the difficulties that you and in the next videos. I will do this exercise with you in two ways. First, with the move absolute and then with a combination of absolute and relative.

PROJECT 2 - CARRIER MOTION - PART 3 - AUTO MODE – MOVEABSOLUTE

As I told you in the previous video. Automatic mode starts at state equal to 20, so. This is where we get into automatic mode. The axes are not moving and we are waiting for the user to press the start button. So over here, I will write a comment saying that this is is where the ultra mode is active and that we are waiting for the start. OK, so state 20. We should check it if we receive a start request, and we can see that by taking a look at our rising trigger function book that we have here and the Q output. And we can see say over here that if you receive a starting request, we should move to another state. So let's say state 30. And if you remember what we did in the previous exercise over here, we have this running flag that is linked to this running Boolean variable and we should set this valuable to true GSX running equal to true. And the results are our that we need to do in this state, that is, we need to handle transition back to the to the manual mode. And if this is done in the same way that we had for the for the fan exercise and we have this state 60, as this done is used to stop the access and transition to the new mode. So over here, we can rally to come and sing transition to manual mode. And we can say that if our machine mode is equal to machine mode that manual, then we should stop the access. So we have this SB stop carrier B stock carrier that executes equal to true. And in this implementation, and this is the same as the first exercise for the stop for the stop function block. We are not specifying at this celebration value because we may want to switch between the deceleration and the emergency deceleration. So we need to ride this when we start stop procedure. So you're our right. FBI top carrier the deceleration equal to deceleration. Celebration. And then we should move to the transition state, so you are state is equal to 60. OK, that is fine. So here we receive our start request and then we move to state 30. So instinctually, we should we have the auto mode active as well, and we should move to position equal to zero.

```
PROGRAM MainProgram
VAR
    uiState            : UINT;
    rtStart            : R_TRIG;

    fbPowerCarrier          : MC_Power;
    fbMoveAbsoluteCarrier   : MC_MoveAbsolute;
    fbMoveRelativeCarrier   : MC_MoveRelative;
    fbStopCarrier           : MC_Stop;
    fbJogCarrier            : MC_Jog;
    fbReadActualPosition    : MC_ReadActualPosition;
    fbReadActualVelocity    : MC_ReadActualVelocity;
    fbReadAxisError         : MC_ReadAxisError;
    fbReset                 : MC_Reset;
END_VAR

//***********************************************
//*** AUTO MODE - WRITE YOUR CODE HERE ***

//*** Auto Mode Action - Wait For Start
0:
    // Start Segment
    IF rtStart.Q THEN
        uiState := 10;
        G_bRunning := TRUE;
    END_IF

    // Transition to Manual Mode
    IF G_etMachineMode = ET_MachineMode.Manual THEN
        fbStopCarrier.Execute := TRUE;
        fbStopCarrier.Deceleration := G_lrDeceleration;
        uiState := 40;
    END_IF

//*** Auto Mode Action - Move to Position
10:

//*************************************************
//*** Transition Manual --- Auto
40:
    IF fbStopCarrier.Done THEN
```

And how can we do that, we can do that with the move absolute. And in order to do so, we need to. Use the move, absolute function Block said its target position and target velocity, because over here, let me see. You're for the move. Absolutely. We are not currently setting any velocity and we need to start the movement. So I will say over here that the move absolute caviar. That execute should be equal to. So we start a movement that be moved by absolute carrier, that positions should be equal to zero because we are moving to a zero position and then we move absolute carrier dot. Velocity should be equal to the global viable JLR carrier target velocity. OK, this is nice. Then here. We should handle different transitions, so the main point is that we need to check if the function block the move, absolute career is finished. So I will say that we have reached the target position, position reached. If we have the move, absolute career that then. OK, so if we have this, we should reset the move the carrier execute the falls in order to allow for the function block to reset. And moved to another state. Let's say you are a state equal to 40. OK, then we need to handle other transitions in the state, so we need to handle the transition to manual mode so we can copy this code here and paste it down here because we may want to transition to manual mode, even if we are if we are in the state. And we need to make sure that they execute and put the move absolutely set the force as well, so we will carry this line here and here. And since we are running right now, we need also to handle a transition to stop the cycle, so if someone presses the stop button. So over here I will also write. Stop request.

```
PROGRAM MainProgram
VAR
    uiState                 : UINT;
    rtStart                 : R_TRIG;

    fbPowerCarrier          : MC_Power;
    fbMoveAbsoluteCarrier   : MC_MoveAbsolute;
    fbMoveRelativeCarrier   : MC_MoveRelative;
    fbStopCarrier           : MC_Stop;
    fbJogCarrier            : MC_Jog;
    fbReadActualPosition    : MC_ReadActualPosition;
    fbReadActualVelocity    : MC_ReadActualVelocity;
    fbReadAxisError         : MC_ReadAxisError;
    fbReset                 : MC_Reset;
END_VAR
```

```
//*** Auto Mode Active - Move to Position = 0
30:
        fbMoveAbsoluteCarrier.Execute := TRUE;
        fbMoveAbsoluteCarrier.Position := 0;
        fbMoveAbsoluteCarrier.Velocity := G_lrCarrierTargetVelocity;

        // Position Reached
        IF fbMoveAbsoluteCarrier.Done THEN
            fbMoveAbsoluteCarrier.Execute := FALSE;
            uiState := 40;
        END_IF


        // Transition to Manual Mode
        IF G_etMachineMode = ET_MachineMode.Manual THEN
            fbMoveAbsoluteCarrier.Execute := FALSE;
            fbStopCarrier.Execute := TRUE;
            fbStopCarrier.Deceleration := G_lrDeceleration;
            uiState := 60;
        END_IF


        ///////////////////////////////////////////
        //*** Transition Manual --- Auto
        40:
```

So if we have a stop request, the Surjeet ex stop, but then what we should do, we should set the Boolean flag. The running flag to falls because we are not working right now and we need to call a stop function clock. So we will have this stuff carrier that execute equal to true beast of carrier the deceleration equal to allow the celebration. Then again, we need to make sure that the execute of the move absolutely is set to false. So again, I woke up with this line over here and we need to transition to a state that will use to wait for this stopping procedure to be finished. And let's say that this is state 50. So. Here we will have the photo and state 50. And as I was saying, a state 50 is the state in which we have. The auto mode active and we are stopping. So over here simply, we will look at. We'll take a look to see if we are done stopping. And also, we need to wait for the button to not be pressed anymore.

So I will write it if this stuff carrier the Don and not the Jeep stop. Then I can set the execute of the stock to false. And we can move back to state 20 in which we are waiting for the start. And this shall be our stopping state. So is the 30 we are handling. A moment from a certain position that may be whatever, because we may have moved the axis manual mode and maybe whatever, we are moving to zero, then in the next state we shall be moving the axis to the target position that is written in this valuable. And actually, the code is pretty much the same. So you're I'll write a comment saying this is auto mode and I would not actively move. Let me see what I wrote. Move to target position. And I can't simply copy this code. Over here. Based it down here. I need to change in the target position. The air carrier target position. And what should we do when we finish this movement, when this movement is finished, we shall move back to zero. So since State 30 is the one way in which we are moving to zero, I can simply set this transition back to state 30. Let me see, and let's go online and try it out. Let's start. Let's get into our visualization over here. Let's. Wait for four to respond. And let's click on Enable. Let's set some values here, and let's see hand ready in order to make it not to slow and hundred as a target position. Manual mode and I can't move it. Let's see if the transition works. Back to manual mode. And let's get back to our top. And let's start. We are getting to zero. And moving forward and backward, we can see over here the state bouncing between 30 and 40 and a less change. The target and this should take place, so when we get back to state 40. So if we wait 1000. You can see that right now we are in 40 and moving forward. And then we get to state 30 moving backward. Let me change the velocity to 200. And at the start of the next movement, we should move faster. Exactly. Let's try this stop. OK, we stop. Let's start again. Stop again. Start again. Rest stop when we are moving forward. We start moving backward. OK, so you can see that this was pretty simple. And we were able to use the move absolute to carry out movement. So remember? Move absolute excited to start it for without raising triggers and check the down output to see if we have finished. My suggestion is typically that you should do this. It is pretty much simpler to read in a single state. So in this way, I'm I'm setting this at target to throw at each cycle that you can see that I have the single movement in a single state. So often I like to do things in this way.

FINAL PROJECT – INTRODUCTION

We will start to see the next exercise for this cause that is about independent motion for multiple acts as you can fight the project or project archive, file the attachments of this lesson. And in this video, we will discuss what you will find inside the project once you open it. So if you open the project, you will find, first of all. Simulation folder over here. And this is a set of people use the app to handle the simulation of the process. Over here in the project and he should not write any code in there, you should simply leave it alone as he knows it will handle some aspects of the simulations and you will find a single set of global variables or here that you will use to interact with sensors and each mys, as always. For the full project, you will find a mean program that in your case will be empty, in which you will write your own code and, as always, a visualization for the process. So. Let's take a look at what this problem is, what this process is and how you can address it. This is a multiple access project. You can see that you have three axis that are two conveyors, an infinite conveyor and outfit conveyor and then a pusher axis. So in this project, you will have to conveyors. Some kind of products will spawn at the beginning of the conveyor. Your goal is to get them in this position where you have this piston or this pusher axis that you will use to push the products onto the second conveyor. And from the second conveyor, you will move them out and they will the product and the products will appear on the first conveyor in not in an orderly manner, but they were up here at random times and you will need to make them order it in the second conveyor. And it will be much easier for me to show you what I mean. But first, let's take a look at the axis.

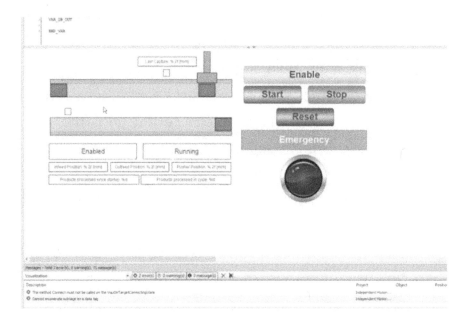

So since conveyors can run, let's say, for an indefinite amount of time in a specific axis, you will have both conveyors as modular axis with a 550 mm model and two axis are the same. So this was a mistake. This is five fifty and. The pusher axis is a finite axis with some software limits, but actually you will see that you will only need to move it from zero to 100. And. I will show you how it works. So let's go online, we did download and I will show you how the complete process should work out. So first of all, the interface is a little bit different that you only have a few buttons over here, you will only have an automatic mode, so you will have a button to enable the access and a feedback here saying that he access are enabled. You do not have a manual mode, so you will not be able to jog the access. We're a steelworks, you have all the positions of the axis. You have some counters for the process, for the product, and you will be able to start to stop the automatic cycle, some start an emergency and reset it. You will also not be able to set the dynamic parameters for the movement in the body. To me, this is not the goal of the project since we have already seen that in previous exercises over here, you will use the fixed parameters that are set in the global variables. So I will just show you how this works must first, and I think over here you have two sensors, one sensor that is on the first conveyor on the inside conveyor to detect products, a proximity sensor and a second one that is at the end of the second conveyor. This one is simply used to count the products that you have processed. We have two counters, one that will never reset, and that is the number of products that are being processed since the machine has been switched on and the counter that this counting just that the number of products that have been processed in this cycle.

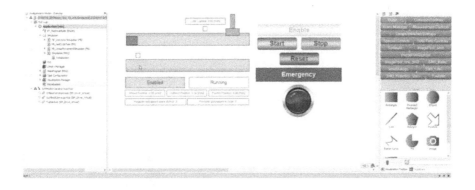

So this will reset once you stop and restart the machine. Just one thing about this sensor, this sensor is actually faster sensor. It means that will capture the exact position of the infant conveyor axis when a product is detected here. So your goal should be that when you detect the product here, you will know what the position of the conveyor was. So you will know. How much you need to move to get a products exactly on the position you need it to be. So let me start it to show you how it works. These are products being generated in a random way. The pusher will push one on the second conveyor, and you can see that the second conveyor won't move in move velocity fashion in a continuous motion. It will simply move it by a specific distance in order to allow for the products to be equally spaced. And you can see that on this sensor, you will get a value that is actually millimeters and that is about the conveyor position. The computer access position when the product was detected. So you will use this to end this second movement. And as you can see right now, we are getting some products here and they are being counted over here. And this is how the main process should work. Before we start writing, could I suggest you think about it and to think about what you could do to reach this, this result and with the function blocks that we studied in the course? Also, I will show you that if you stop. All the access will stop with some deceleration. And as you saw the completed, the conveyors are cleared of all the products. And if you start again, you will need to reposition the pusher to the initial position. And. In the same manner, if you have an emergency. The axis will stop in a much faster way so that the deceleration will be bigger will be different. And then in order to reset the emergency, you will need to remove it, reset and start again. So these are the requirements for the product. Sorry for the project, and also you can see here that this counter has not been reset that while this one has. So let's take a look at the global variable list now.

So the global variables that you can use it, we all need to use that to interact with the simulation. So here you will have them divided into two repositories a global variable repositories and the global constant repository. So the constant ones will mostly be parameters and the geometric features of the process. Instead, here you will have a feedbacks. So sensors from the machine and some of our most 48. So starting here, he will have the enable start stop, reset and emergency buttons. You will have the slides that you have on the machines so enabled and running it and the alarm. You will have the feedbacks that you need to to complete for the actual position of the axis and the counters for the products that have been processed. Then you will have the two sensors. So actually here you will have the proximity and outfit. This is this one at the end of the outfit conveyor and you have the first sensors in the feed conveyor that is this one. And you will find it whenever this gets set to true. Over here, you will actually find the new capture of the of the infield can be your access position. Then looking at the constants, you will have three dynamic parameters that will need you will need to use for all the axis. So each axis will have the same acceleration, deceleration and emergency the separation. You will have the velocities for the three axis. You will always need to use this one and you will not need to change it. This is a consent with the product size, so the product size is the product is actually

50 millimeters wide. This is actually not of many. You will not use this, but it's good to know.

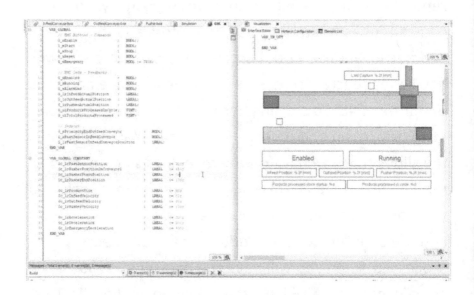

You will have heard the start and end position of the pusher. So the pusher will need to be here when the first thing hear is moving. And this is something that you will need to handle and that we need to get to 100 to move the products onto the next conveyor. Then you have the position of both the sensor here means that when this becomes true, when the censor becomes through, the product should be at 300 mm onto the conveyor. And this is the position for a product to be onto the future position. So theoretically, at least once you get this to true, you should move off another one hundred and fifty millimeters. Actually, you won't need that to. It won't be enough to just wait for the sensor to come through because you may have travelled a little bit more. So a good way is to use this cap tour. So I will let you think about it and you will see how to use it when we will be writing the code for this project. So. This is what he should do and what you have. To work on the three axis, we know the function blocks of the PRC, open standard soft motion codes this library, we can use a fun and in next week we will tackle this problem and this we will reach exactly this result.

FINAL PROJECT - MOTION CONTROL FUNCTION BLOCK DECLARATION

So let's start the software development process for this project, the. Right now, we will have the most boring part of the project because we will need to to instantiate the end, the call or the all the motion control and function blocks that are needed for this project. So first, that we will need to declare them over here and also create a motion control action to call or the functions. So let's first do that, so over here, I will likely continue the program. Create an action instructor texted that I will call motion control costs. And into the main program implementation, I will write. That's right, a comment saying that this is motion control calls and. Motion control calls. So we will be calling this action here and in the action we will call all the function looks. OK, so we need to think about what are the function blocks that we need in order to carry out this process. So let's start from the administrative and diagnostics functional blocks. Surely we will need to power on all three axes, so let's create over a year and see power for all the axes. So I would create an SB power in field conveyor AFB power outfit conveyor. FBI power pusher. And the type of this will be power. Then. We will need to have some diagnostics in the case of errors, so I will need a FBI read axis error for each axis. So let me copy this right in feed conveyor then. Have be relaxed, etc. outfit conveyor and be relaxed, etc. pusher, any type will be M.C. read at this hour. The errors, we will also need to be able to reset them as. If it conveyor be reset outfit conveyor and FBI reset pusher and the type will be MCU reset. Then moving on, we will also need to read the actual position of the axis, so have be read act to a position in seat conveyor. So let me copy this the first part of the name of the function book and that outfit the conveyor and pusher. And this will be read actual position. And I think for the purpose of this project, these are the main administrative or diagnostic function books that we need order to read errors. We set them and read the position of the axis, you know, so power them on. OK, so this is fine for us. Now we need to think about the motion.

Control function books are actually the function book that will be moving the access. So first of all, it doesn't matter what we will be doing with them. Surely we will need to be able to stop them. So we will need an AMC stop for each axis.

And I will write them down here. So be stuck, stuck, say conveyor b stop outfit conveyor at b stop pusher and the type. Let me close, the visitation for now will be an easy stop. Then let me think about what we need to do, so as soon as the product appears on the conveyor, we will need to move the country forward. So this will be a continuous motion until we reach this sensor, so we will need move velocity for the conveyor, for the feed conveyor. Then once we get to this position, we will need to move the axis by a certain distance. And in order to do this, we will need the move. Relative function lo For the future, we will only need to move it between zero and 100 to the known position that we have in this global Constance. So since this are absolute values of position for the axis, we will only need to move absolute for this axis. Then once we move the product onto the outfit conveyor, we will need again to move the conveyor by a known distance. And again, this will be a move relative. So to recap, we will need to move velocity for the infield move relative for the infield and move absolute for the pusher and a move relative for the outfit. So let's get back to our program and we'll open the visualization. You're on the right. Sorry, let me do this this way. So below. So I have all the space to write the function books. So as I said, we need a move velocity, a single move velocity only for the infinite. So a right move, velocity and fit. AMC movie Velocity. I will need a move, relative. But for the infield and for the outfield, so be move relative. You'll see it. Sorry, it's 18 feet conveyor. So you see the conveyor here and FBI move relative outfit conveyor. And this will be NMC, well, relative, then we need to move absolute only for the push beat move. Absolutely push. I'm see the absolute. And this function blocks should be enough for us. And now let's get to the most boring part that this to actually call them all. In a consistent way in our motion control costs action. So let's get in here. I will open the program on the right and I will write a comment here.

Seeing in feed, convey your name, CFB calls. So I will have to be power infill conveyor. Here I will add the axis that is in conveyor in equal to true stable. So if it can be your axis is the name of the axis in the project. This is one then. After the second one, we need to relax is the error. Let me read this error. You see the conveyor. This will be in feed conveyor access and I will also leave this equal. This enable equal to truth. So we will always read the errors. Then we have the reset, be resetting the conveyor. Here I will have an infinite conveyor axis and we will manage the reset. Let's say in a naive way. But this is often the way to do this and it's simpler so we can simply move. We can simply set the execute of the reset equal to the reset button. This is something that is often often done. We want to look at the outcome of the reset operation. We just want to make sure that when we reset something, we send a reset to the to the axis. So here I would write. GSX Reset. OK, then moving on here we have the f to be reactor position. The axis is the same. Enable should be equal to true. And then we will. Also set the value. Ask the. Gathering feedback, the position was simply right this over here. So we went one check for the valid output, and this is fine. It works in the same way. So let's move on to the stop, so be stop food conveyor. We will set the axis equal to the same one, and we won't set any celebration because we need to switch between the deceleration in the emergency, the situation according to the needs of our stop.

OK, then our press have to again, this we will need right now. The movie velocity has to be move velocity. That's placed the axis here. Let's ask called the velocity here, do you see a large increase, the velocity, the global constant? And let's also record the acceleration and deceleration. We cannot call the deceleration in here because we will never use the emergency declaration in here. We will only use it on the stop function block. And then we have. The FBI will relative. And again, we will use the same access. Same velocity. This acceleration and deceleration. We will not accord any distance because it will may change according to the captor that we have in the process. OK, so we actually. Wrote all the function book calls for the infant conveyor. So let's play it smart and let's do some copy and paste and replace 40 lb ft conveyor. So I will copy of birth control. They control c move down here and write Control V. So we have copied and pasted all the calls we press. Control H and I will replace and fit come here so I can change just in fit to outfit. And I will do manual replacement in order to avoid replacing something that I care about over here. So replace. And I will keep on going, keep on replacing. Oh, sorry. Not until the end, because otherwise I will get to the beginning. We go to the beginning. Let's take a look and see if everything is fine. We need to remove the maximum velocity call because we do not have this function. Look for the outfit conveyor and.

Let's double check if we have all the function books, the power, the Reid axis and the reset reductive position.

The stop. And the move relatively OK, this is fine, and let's play it smart again. That's based this again and control eight, replace and feed conveyor. With Pusher. For next, let's replace one by one. And then we will come back to see. What we missed. Sorry, not. OK, so we do not have a relative and we do not have more velocity. So actually, we only copied the. The diagnostics in a new strategic function looks we need to add the absolute code. So here have to. Have been move absolute. Well, sure, the access will be pusher axis here, GC, do you see a our. Pusher. Velocity. Do you see a lot of acceleration, you see a la. Deceleration. And we do not need to use the direction because this is a finite Texas. And this should be fine for us.

FINAL PROJECT - ENABLING PROCEDURE

Now that we have written that the code regarding the cause of our motion control function, we can get back to the main program and start to write some code for the execution of the task related to the project. So first of all, let's write some comments or here in order to subdivide our valuables. So this hour, Ms. S. Administrative plus diagnostics function looks. This hour, AMC movement function blocks. And let's see other variables. So we will need. A state variable, so let's call the UI state Typekit should be. You didn't then we have many kind of conditions that we need to catch during our code execution, so typically we will need to see the rising trigger, the rising edge of sensors and buttons. So over here we would also need some our Trig.. So I would write Artie, start Artie, stop Artie for the first sensor and Artie for the end sensor. And all of this should be our trick.

And let's call them all at the beginning of our goods rising trigger calls. Right, if you are to start to stop off to Artie fast sensor. To avoid and censor. This will be linked to the global variable G start. This one will be to stop. This one will be TJX first sensor Enfield Conveyor. And this will be its proximity and outfield conveyor. Can see the variable over here. So with this rising triggers, we will have the information on whether or not a rising edge of one of these inputs happened. So let's start to write our state machine. So case you are state off and we will start from state zero. That for us will be our machine visible state. So in this condition, what we would need to do is to wait for the enabled enable button to be pressed and then we will enable the access. But first, in order to make it a little bit more easier to read.

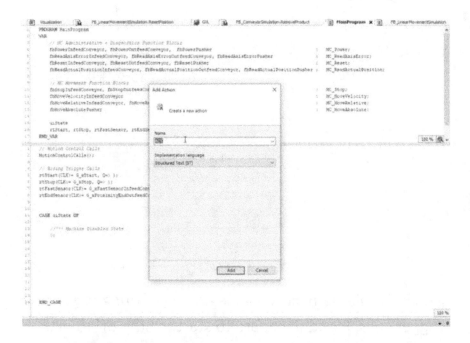

Let's create an action that I will call power on axis. In which we will set all the variables needed to power on all of the axis, and let's create another one called the power of access. So in the power run action, we'll need to set the inputs for the power that we have in the code to true. So where we write is F.B. power in feed conveyor, that right start equal to true. And then we need to do the same for. The other AMC powers, so here, although the same for the outfit and the same for the pusher. And we will need to also set the input. That is called beat regulator on for all three function blocks. Then we can do the same. I was here in the other action, must simply setting all these variables to false. Thirty two, false. So in this state, we will need. To. Wait for the G X enable, and let's also say that we need the access to not be in an emergency, so the emergency, because if you recall, we are using negative logic for emergency, so emergency set to false means that an emergency have been requested. If we have this to, we will get our UI state to state in this state, then we will use the state to power on access. And we will see here we will ride power on access and wait for the access to be power done, so we will wait for FBI power if it can be that status and be power outfit convey here that status and FBI power pusher. That states then if we have. These three conditions, we can move to another state. We will say it is state 20.

And this T20 is a state in which all the actors are enabled, and we are. Let's say in automatic mode, and we will wait for the start button to be pressed. Also, in these two states, we need to handle the. These three leads that we have, so we can safely say right here that he stayed zero, all of them will be false. So GSX enabled should be false. X running should, should be false as well, and x alarm lady should be false. Then. As soon as the axes are enabled, we can see that GSX enabled should be equal to true. Then let's also manage the transition backward, so when the enable input is set to false. And since this transition can occur, no matter the state in which we are, we should we can choose to code this transition outside of our state machine. So here our right to come and saying that this is the disabled transition. My suggestion is typically for state machine to avoid being too many transition outside the machine, but in this case it's it's not too many, so it's fun.

So I would write if not geeks enable it doesn't matter which state we are, we will call the power of axis action and then get back to state zero. So we can try this. Let's go on the line with your download. Let's start the policy. Get into the visualization. We need to wait a few seconds in order to have it respond to our inputs. They enable this for a second.

It started, you can see that the access become enabled. If I remove the enable it become disabled. Let's take a look at it while also looking at our state machine. So that's disable, OK, where is the zero hour public status this false press enables? It becomes Tony because it goes to 10 and then to 20, and our status is true. So we are successfully managing the enabling of more access.

FINAL PROJECT - START AUTOMATIC CYCLE

So I would write that if the artists start the queue is true, then we will move to St.. Tony? And we also will set the ex running through. OK, so what is the first thing that we would need to do once we get in the machine running? One thing could be that we start moving the conveyor forward, but actually the first thing that we need to make sure is for the pusher access to be at a starting position. So what I would do over here, I will say that we are now to mode and I will do a pusher. Repositioning, so if the pusher is already at zero position, it will move. It will not move, but if it isn't, it will move to zero. So we should use the f b move. Our absolute push were not execute equal to true while setting the move absolute that position equal to zero. Then if we have to move absolute pusher, not done. We should reset the move, obviously, to execute two falls and get to state 40. OK, so this is fine. This is the first step, then we should think about what the conveyor needs to do, so we will need to start moving in a continuous mode.

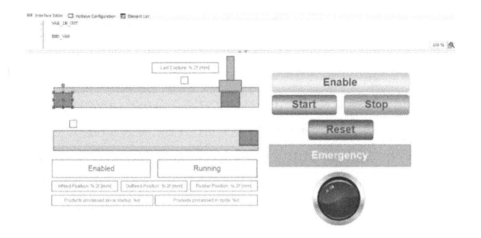

So velocity should occur until we get a capture, so we get this sensor becoming through. And after this becomes true, we should not stop and we can command and move relative from this position to. This position plus a certain amount. So. Let's get the state 40. First of all, we would need to have instead for the start of velocity in feed conveyor. And here with the right, be more velocity in faith, convey your daughter execute equal to true. And we do not need to rate the velocity because we hardcoded it. Here in the call of the move velocity over here. So get him back here. I would simply wait for the conveyor to be in velocity. Sort move. Velocity and velocity then and once we are in velocity, we are moving, I can set the execute the function, look at the falls. And the UI State 250. Then. In state 50, we should. Wait, so auto mode, we should wait for the sensor captures. And we can say this thing. If R T for sensor the Q, then your state can become 60, and in states 16, we can command and move relative. So they start move, relative. If it conveyor. And. In order to do that, if be move relative, it can be or that executes should be equal to true. Then. We should set the the distance for the move relative, and we could simply ride since. This position is 450. This position is one hundred and fifty. Sorry, 300. We can write the difference between these two, since this is the amount of millimeters that we need to move. So I could simply be right here. DCL, our pusher position and conveyor one minus g c l r fast sensor position. So it's straight out is equal to see our pusher position and can be your one minus GC. Hello. I'm sorry. It was fast sensor position. Again, the velocities are accorded the function of so we do not need to write anything more. And I would write if more relative in feed, not done. Then. If the move relative in feet convey you're sorry, this is conveyor. That done and so executed should be equal to false. Why state should be 70, and we wrote quite a few lines of codes, lines of code so we can test them out.

And see what happens. Let's download and we will take a look and see if the conveyor stops at the correct position. So. Let's get to our visualization. Let's enable the access. And for a start, we should have first the repositioning of the pusher. And this is already fine. We are already at the position zero within them, so we will need to. But. Let's see if I better start, see the convoy you're moving. We get the sensor. OK, we stopped. It's almost fine. You can see that we are. If we zoom. Sorry. Let me try to zoom here. We can see that. Yeah, it's fine. But we are not exactly in the position that we expected to because actually the capital was at 300. Let me see what is our current position. You see, that is 450 and not 84. And actually the correct positions would be 450. You could say that this error is negligible, but we do not want it to be negligible. And let's think about what the issue is over here. So there are two main issues. The first one is that we are not using the CAPTCHA, so we are just using the Boolean value from the sensor and we are checking it at the PRC time. So at the task time, and actually we could have a more precise measurement from this fast input. And the second issue here is that we are moving one cycle later than our sense of it.

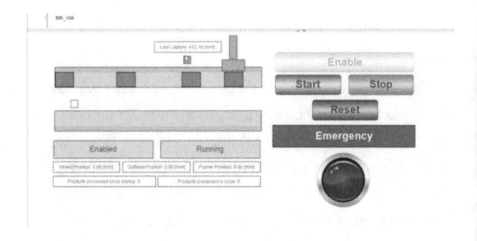

So actually, we read the sensor when we are in state 15, we move to the next state and we command the move relative, then on the next cycle. So actually, we also move. We were also postponed the move of one cycle, so we would gain something by moving this line over here, like this line of code. But actually, we would need to do something more because if we maintain this kind of code, as you can see here, while we had. Our product here. We already got another capture. And actually, if we maintain this kind of state machine, we actually missed this, Artie. So what would happen is that next time we get here, we would not use this product over here because we missed the AH, tweak. So this kind of management for the for the first sensor is not good at all. And it's not good because we are we will miss some products and it's not good because we are not very precise. So let's think about what we can do, actually what we we can do is to create a queue. We will create a queue in which we will write all the captcha measurement that we that we get in the way we would fill a queue whenever we get a sense or read and we will empty the queue. One, we need to move to the correct position for the conveyor.

FINAL PROJECT - CAPTURE MARK DEVELOPMENT

The strategy for managing the first sensor isn't good. We can make it better and in order to the better, we will create a fast sensor capital cue and it will be a five four cue. So first in, first out in order to get our, let's say, our set of values. So we should define that the maximum number of values of capital that we can cue and we will create an array for this. So we create a bar constant here that I will see UI Max number of cute. Captures. And this will be an unsigned integer, and let's say five, even if in our visualization here it gets in the space, we will only have at maximum to see two possible products, but let's say five. Then we will need to create a new way. So I will call ELR first sensor captures that will be an hour that goes from one to this constant that we declared. See, you are max. No, sorry, it isn't. The autocomplete doesn't work here, so it was simply copied. Is of long real. Hello. I will also need to keep track of how many captured so I have queued. So you are a number of captors. You and. So. Here we should. Write some code that is outside the state machine because we want to fill this captors, regardless of the state in which we are. So here I will write that I'll read some code to managing to manage the the minute adding sensor value to captors. Q. And this is done by checking if we have the first sensor our trigger does. Q So if we have this first sensor, our trick, the Q, we will need to add it to the queue. So let's first spend it a few a few times a little amount of time on how this queue should be. So.

What about this should work? So we have an array of five, five long reel, so something like this. Let's use my paint skills to do so. So. What happens when once and we have a same number of captors? And. At the beginning, we will have all zeros, so once we get a new captures, the number of captures will increment and we will have a value here. So let's say that is 300 zero. So this is what happens when we get a capture. Let's say that we get another one. And the captors become, too. We will need to write. In the next Q and in Q value 450, that's a new capital value. So this is what happens when it fails, so we will need to first increment the number of captors so you are no, the captors should be equal to its south plus one. And we will right that the air if a sensor captures of you. You are a number of captors should be equal to the value that ends up. In this Bible. So in this way, we will store new values. For the third sensor captor. So in this way, we will not have. Any problem with the losing values?

But. Actually, we need also to, let's say, do something about both removing the values from the queue. And also, we will need to. Actually manage this distance in a more clever way. So. First, let's take a look on how to remove the key, the value from the queue, so. We will need to do that when the move relative is finished. So here I will write some code to remove the cap to the we used from the list. Lost and actually, we will always use the. The first cell of the array because. It is the first one that occurred. And so sorry, and I think here here, we do not need to wait for the artifact sense of the queue. But we simply just need to wait for the number of captors to be bigger than zero because this part of the code here with manage that. So here I will need to remove the capital from the list only if once they've finished the move relative. So how does this work? What should happen? Well, we would need to decrement this value. And. More of this value. So let's zoom it out. We will need to move this value to here. And right. Zero here. So what we can how can we achieve this? Well, we can say that UI number of captures is equal to UI number of captures when the Sun. Then we can make a full lo So we need a value valuable to use as index for a for loop out of this index. So. For UI Index is equal to one two, you are number of captures the. We will need to set the value of the cell to the value of the next cell of the array. And I will write so I will write a lot of first sensor captures a few high number of captures equal to hail our first sensor captures of UI number of characters plus one.

And then I would need to set the first sensor captures of UI number of characters plus one plus one because I documented it here, I remember the one value over a year. So this will become equal to zero. So these are the five lines of code to remove a character from the. From the queue, so we added to the queue. We removed the value from the queue. Actually, we need to use this vetting for the queue. And how can we use this? So. Actually, in order to correct our movement, we would need to know how much the excess moved from the position that it had when it reached the sensor. So. What we can do is create a viable. That I will call our fast sensor difference. This will be a long real. And I can say that this alarm fast sensor difference should be equal to. The actual position of the axis so that in convey your axis. That. I can use the set position because in virtual mode, this is the same. So we're at a set position, so this is the target position that has been set to the axis. But let's say we can ease the actual sorry, this is the same for us. So the actual position of the axis. And we can use this on the axis or in a better way. We can use the longer evil ones, so Jill are in federal position. Minus. The value from the captor, so alar, fast captures of one. So this is actually the position in which we are now now that we are commanding the move relative minus the position that we had. When we captured the value that should be around that, that 0.84 that we saw previously. And then we can subtract this value over here, four cents or difference. So let's go online and tried. Oh, sorry, I don't know if we actually set this value in the motion control cost less. Let me see. You. It seems that we do. So let's go online. Sensation. And it to reopen. And let's see how it works. Enable. Start. So the capture occurs at 300, OK? There's something wrong here. We are moving forward. Let me see what happens. OK, we got something weird here, OK? This is actually zero and it is actually zero because let me see. Down here.

This should not be zero. Let me see why this. Yeah, we made a mistake because we are writing this in feed. Also for the pusher, I guess so we have heard the reductio position that is ear for the outfit that goes on to the outfit, but for the pusher goes on to the infield. So this is the mistake. So this is pusher. Act opposition. OK, let's get it back online and try it again. So let's enable start and let's see what happens. And you got to capture. And actually, we stopped at a better position this is for 50 to 24. And in this way, we are actually using the stored value of the capital. Actually, this is not very precise because we have some communication. Say issue, whether we may have some communication issue or slow down. But actually in this way, if we use the capital, we are much faster because we are not relying on the policy cycle time and on the velocity of the input electronically, but we are relying on something that is more fast. So actually, we built this and you will see that this is actually useful for when we get to multiple cycles. But actually, there is just one modifications that we need because this is our modular position. So in some cases, you may have another flow a rollover. Sorry. So let's say that you so your position can range between zero and 550 if you get a capture just below the rollover. And when we did this measurement, the rollover already happened. For instance, you may get here five sorry here. Five hundred and forty nine and you may get here one. And because you have rolled over. So actually, if you do this here, you will get a negative value. So one minus five hundred and forty nine. So we need to manage the rollover. So here will be managed rollover. And we can say simply that if our first sensor difference is negative and it should never be negative because we are moving forward, then our first sensor difference should be equal to itself, plus five hundred and fifty. That is the conveyor line in the module of the axis. OK, so this was an important modification, and we will move on for the hour to finish the automatic mode.

FINAL PROJECT - FINISH AUTOMATIC CYCLE

We actually managed to get the conveyor to stop at the correct position. Then what do we need to do is to move the pusher forward? So we are in state 70. Here and the state is again. And auto mode. And this is when we move push her forward. 70. And in order to do that, we will use the move absolute function lo Moves absolute that executes equal to truth be move absolute pusher. That. Position should be equal to a constant that we have a GCR posture and position actually in order to make it more modular, more consistent. We should right here instead of zero GC. Hello. Push start position. It is actually zero. But since we have a constant value for that, it is better to do it this way. And here I would write it. If they move absolute finishes then or UI states become 80. And we should. We should also reset our Move episode, execute the False.

```
        fbStopInfeedConveyor, fbStopOutfeedConveyor, fbStopPusher         :   MC_Stop;
        fbMoveVelocityInfeedConveyor                                      :   MC_MoveVelocity;
        fbMoveRelativeInfeedConveyor, fbMoveRelativeOutfeedConveyor       :   MC_MoveRelative;
        fbMoveAbsolutePusher                                              :   MC_MoveAbsolute;

        uiState                                                           :   UINT;
        rtStart, rtStop, rtFastSensor, rtEndSensor                        :   R_TRIG;

        aiFastSensorCaptured                                              :   ARRAY [1.._uiMaxNumberOfQueueCaptures] OF LREAL;
        uiNumberOfCaptures                                                :   UINT;
        uiIndex                                                           :   UINT;
        lrFastSensorDifference                                            :   LREAL;
    END_VAR
    VAR CONSTANT
        c_uiMaxNumberOfQueueCaptures                                      :   UINT     := 5;
    END_VAR

            // Remove capture from the list
            uiNumberOfCaptures := uiNumberOfCaptures - 1;
            FOR uiIndex := 1 TO uiNumberOfCaptures DO
                aiFastSensorCaptures[uiNumberOfCaptures] := aiFastSensorCaptures[uiNumberOfCaptures + 1];
            END_FOR
            aiFastSensorCaptures[uiNumberOfCaptures + 1] := 0;

            uiState := 50;
        END_IF

        (**** Auto Mode - Move Pusher Forward
        50:
            fbMoveAbsolutePusher.Execute := TRUE;
            fbMoveAbsolutePusher.Position := 0d_lrPusherEndPosition;
            IF fbMoveAbsolutePusher.Done THEN
                fbMoveAbsolutePusher.Execute := FALSE;
                uiState := 60;
            END_IF

    END_CASE

    // Disable Operation
    IF NOT D_xEnable THEN
```

OK, so the pusher should move forward, and then instead, 18, we should move the pusher backward. And we will also need later to move the conveyor, this conveyor forward and actually the distance that we need to move it forward, that should be actually a little bit bigger than the product size. And we will see how that actually we can do this movements all at once in order to save time. So here I will write auto mode, move pusher backwards and both feed conveyor forward so I could copy this code here for what concerns the pusher. And the only difference is that we need to move back to the start position. Then we need to do the same for the career to move relative forward for the. Outfield can be so moving relative that with the conveyor that executes

186

should be equal to true be move relative to field conveyor. That distance should be equal to, let's say, the size of the product. So GC our product size plus five. Let's see. And then we should move to the next state. Once we got both the move relative. Of the outfit conveyor and the move that suit the pusher, the. So we will set also. The FBI move, relative.

In fact, outfit conveyors, sorry, outfit conveyor that execute equal to false. And then we will get to the U.S. state. Actually, we finished our cycle because we moved the product over a year, pushed it down, pushed the second conveyor and that the pusher moved back. So actually, we can begin the cycle again from the position of moving the conveyor. So.

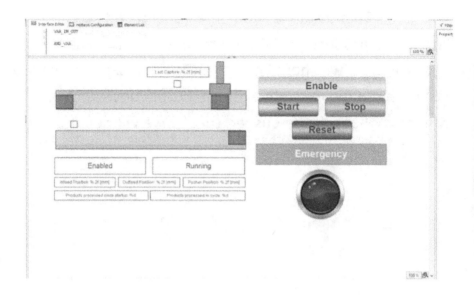

We could simply. Get down here and get to. State 40, the pusher is already at the initial position, so we don't need to go to 30. We can get to state 40 in which we start the conveyor. We see if the captors. Are are present. We have seen captures. And so on. So here I can simply say. That we can get the state photo. OK, so let's try it out by going online with a download. So we are here online. That's enabled start. And let's see if it works fine. Yup. It seemed to work fine. And as you can see, we managed to also handle the second product that was captured while at the conveyor was moving at relative. So actually, it seemed to work out fine, and we need to manage a few things, we will need to manage this sensor in order to increment the values of the counters. And we will also need to manage the stop in emergency buttons. So first, let's go offline and. Manage the counters.

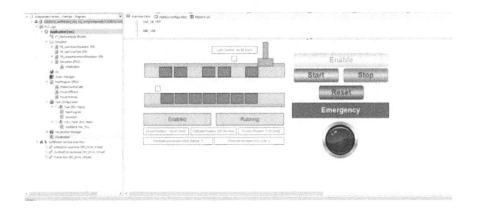

So this is pretty easy, so we need to get back at the beginning of our code and say that if we get a rising figure of yes sir the queue, then we can increment both the the counters. So there are global. So the first one is D.U.I. products processed in cycles, so this would be equal to itself plus one. And the second one DUI to the products would be again equal to its a one. Now the only difference between these two is that this one. So the one in the cycle needs to be reset it when we start a new cycle so we can. Do that. When we start the machine, so when we get an early start, this is equal to zero. Actually, we go online right now, we can see we should be able to see them. Incrementing themselves so well, actually right now, we have no mean to stop the the access. So actually, we will only see them get bigger and bigger..

FINAL PROJECT - STOP AND EMERGENCY REACTIONS

We managed to successfully complete the automatic part that automatic cycle of the machine. Right now, we will need to take care of the stop procedures and the emergency stop procedures. So in order to do that, let's first create some actions that will make our life easier. So whenever we stop the access or also when we power of the access in the disabled transition here, we would need to do two things. First of all, since all of our products will disappear from the visualization, we will need to clear our cue list and we will need to do that when we disable, when we stop and when we emergency stop. So this is something that we will do quite a few number of times. So let us create an action for that. So action and I will call this clear captures cues captured. Q.

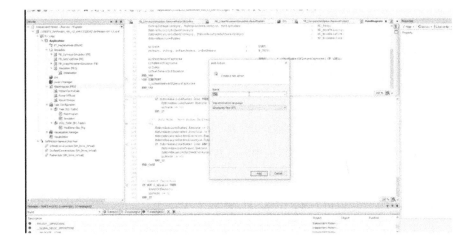

And in order to do that, we can use a for loop saying for you index, we already have the variable in the view from this value to the number of computers that we have stored. Let's set the value to zero. And then set the number of characters. Two zero as well. Then I thing that we need to do whenever we disable, when we stop and so on will be to set all the executes of all the function blocks to zero two false. So I would call this to this action disable executes. And in order to do that, we will simply need to set the execute of all the function books that we are using to force. So let me first do something like this. So. I will press the old button and right, not execute. He called the false semicolon. Let's feel the function. Look here. So from the inside, we have the velocity and the move relative. Well, relative in feared. Let me sorry if it can be released, no. The name of the function book, I guess. OK, if it can be here, then we have the has as we stop as well, if it can be. For the outfit, we are sorry for the air, for the outfit, we are all the move relative and the stop. And for the. Pusher, we have the we have the move, absolute pusher and this top pusher. Let's remove these lines. And we are fine. So in our main program here, whenever we disable the axis, we will also add before we will say that we will be disabling, disable able executes and. Clear. Kaspersky. OK, that is fine.

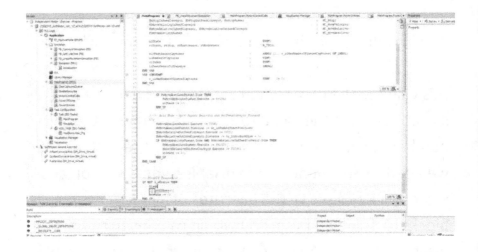

And let's now move on to the emergency stop and to the, let's say, normal stop. OK, so. Let's say that we use that the states. So here we will need to have a state to stop the access so we will command them, see, stop for the access and here we will wait for them to stop stopping the access. And. Then we will need to also have some states for the emergency. So what we will need to do again for the emergency, we will need to do the same thing. So, so state one under these emergency. This would be against stopping the access, then for the emergency. We need also to disable the access so we will have a state to the we will call these enabling the access. This is 110. And here we will have another state emergency. Wait for reset. So actually, we will need three states for the emergency and one for the stopping. So now let's think about what are the conditions for us to get into the states so. That's a virus stop transition, you know, so an emergency transition. So let's see what are the conditions to have this transition? So first of all, we will need to have in there to stop the queue. And we will need to not be already stopped. So actually, for us, it would be state bigger than 20. Because instead, zero, we wouldn't need to do that in state, then we wouldn't need to do that because we are still an institution as well. So let's say that we need the state to be bigger. So UI state to be bigger. The 20, and we do not want to do this when we are in emergency, so let's say lowered and went on, but because this will be the states that we will use for the emergency state lower than 100. Then if we have this conditions, we will need to clear the captures.

And also disable the executes. He's able to execute. Then we will need to. Let me see what what's wrong here? Well, I forgot the then. Then we need to send the execute two through to all the stops to the F, B and C stop, so I would say f b stop and it over your data execute equal to truth and this will be done. Also for the outfit. And the pusher. Pusher, who should. And I will also need to set the deceleration, so be stop and should conveyor that deceleration should be equal to G.R. deceleration. So the sort of GC a lot of deceleration. And this should be true for. Of the axis, so I woke up this two times and. Copy and paste the value of the butcher. To the Bush. And also, since we are stopping, we need to set the running viable, the running to force, and then we can move to a state equal to 80. In the same way here, we will need to manage the transition to the emergency. So here over here, we have more conditions because we are also all the hours. So if? Well, one condition is not emergency, so not emergency. Yes. We do not need. This or we need to stop if also we have an error from the. With access, ever what the function looks, and also we will need to check the software and switch active only for the pusher because it is the only one that has limits. Switches. Software limits. Switches. So here I would write if we have this or if we read access error in feed, can your data error or have be read access error outfit configured at error or be read access error. Not so pusher, not error or the last one is to be read X's error push that s w and switch active then. Sorry. And we also need. So this would be we wouldn't need the parentheses for this. Sorry. Because we will need to have this. So one of these conditions, and we do not need an emergency if the state is zero and we do not need them an emergency of this, we are already handling one. So states should be also lowered and onward. We may need to handle the emergency here because the emergency needs to power it off the axis. So if we have all of this, we can simply copy this code from the start procedure. And. We will need simply to change the deceleration emergency declaration. Emergency authorization and emergency declaration, and we will need to move the state zero. We want the need to set this flag because we will, however, do that. He said zero. No, actually, we need to do that and we need to move to stage one. I'm really sorry that the states you.

So we wrote this asynchronous, let's say, transitions right now we need to write to the states. So these are pretty simple. So we need to write here that if we have here, we are managing the stop. So. If we have the done output of all the function, lo And stop Pusher done. Then we can set the execute the force, be stop, if it can be or execute, this would be false. If we stop outfit convey, your tickets should be false and be stopped. For sure, that executes should be false. And since we stopped that we can go back to the state in which we wait for a new start trigger that estate planning. OK, so the stuff should be managed for the emergency, we need to do something similar. We need to wait for the stop to be to be stopped done to be true, but only after that we will move to stage 110. And another thing we need to do is when we get an emergency, we need to turn emergency light on. So alarm led should be equal to true as well. OK, then in one hundred and ten, we need to do the opposite of what we are doing in state then so we can copy this. We need to disable the access, so I will face this. I will change power and to power off, and I will check for not. For all these variables. Jack's enabled will become false, and then we can move to St. one hundred and twenty. State 120, we can simply say that if if we have reset, then your state should be equal to zero. So the emergency is stop these able reset, and in the meanwhile, if you are an error on the axis, you will send a reset through all the axis. So let's try out.

You start the PRC and go to the visualization. And it will start. That's stop already. That the products are disappearing. Let's start again. It doesn't work. Let me see why. We are still in a state 80. Oh, yeah, that's wrong. We were moving Interstate 80 and we should move to stay 90. So this is a mistake. Let's try again with a download. OK, visualization. Animals start stop. Start again. Stop again. Perfect. It's working. That's right. Stop. You know, at the moment. So let's stop to. Here, this is the possibly the most wrong moment in here. We will understand the value of having this state. State. Turkey, which we do the crucial repositioning. We'll see that starts. First, the pusher goes to the start position, then the conveyor starts. OK, this is great. That's right, an emergency stop. We see that not only the machine becomes not running, but also not enabled. It's fine. Let's remove the emergency reset and start. It works fine as well. Let's leave it going for a while to see if our counters are working in the correct way. So the first one should keep implementing should maintain its value, while the second one should go to zero. Once we stop the automatic cycle. Or Beirut should go to zero when we start a new cycle. So actually, it's fine if it remains equal to the value that it had with the other one. So now it should be counting. We get one on both counters that said, let's say two products.